Thulani Tomose

LIBERATION AFTER
20 YEARS OF WAR
IN MY HEAD

novum ◢ pro

© 2020 novum publishing

ISBN 978-1-64268-139-0
Editing: Karen Simmering
Cover photo: Thulani Tomose
Cover design, layout & typesetting:
novum publishing

www.novumpublishing.com

Liberation after 20 years of war in my head

This is my story, my processing and recognition. I've had several triggers in my life that have put me, my will and my views on life. I used to be afraid to write this book about my life. I was more interested in other people's opinions and will than in my own.

My book isn't suitable for everyone. It is addressed to certain people. I'm writing this book not to convince anybody of anything, but to convince me do it for me and for the people that it will motivate to read how I dealt with my problem and what I did with it and what helped me. Maybe it'll help someone out there with their own problems or to get better prepared for the strokes of fate in life. I'm not the only one who's experienced such harsh situations or is experiencing them at this very moment.

Many do not dare to tell anyone about their personal strokes of fate. This can have many different reasons, which I can understand, because I myself belonged for a long time to this group. But I do want to encourage these people to confide in someone so as not to have to confront their problems alone.

Earlier on I didn't know how I, on my own, could avert this war in my head with all the deep wounds, losses and injuries and liberate my feelings to help myself out. I didn't know how I'd ever get back to myself and to regain the joy of life – after a long time of grave abuses during my childhood. I see myself not as an omniscient counselor or anything. I'm not a writer, I'm still world-famous. I've only got my story I'd like to tell you.

I learned too soon of the cruelty of life and was confronted with adult problems far too early. I had to learn how to handle that. My trust was destroyed too soon, broken by people that I trusted and loved as a child. It wasn't a childhood you would wish for yourself or for others. I've been through this and I learned that I see life through different eyes than most people. I felt extraordinary in my life and today I can understand why.

I want to tell my story openly, just the way it went, without any taboos. Without hurting anyone, though. I want to tell my story the way it went, because it helps if it is not embellished, but just described as it was. Sometimes bad things happen in life. Things we don't have any influence on. You begin to feel lonely, isolated, angry, depressed, cursed, extraordinary.

But here, too, I have found that there's a way to deal with it, if you have the will. It's not easy. It's more liberating than living in the hole of dark thoughts, like I did for 20 years. I've experienced it and I know what it is like to have a traumatized childhood. I know what it means to be sexually and physically abused. I also know what it's like to be forced by fate to cope with the challenges of life, such as losing my own sister to murder by a family member or living through a terrible car accident. I never thought it possible to feel free and delivered from the past. Today I say: It is very sad how I looked at life and myself but there were a lot of reasons why I felt life so gray, hopeless and lustless.

I grew up in different places in South Africa. In the beginning I lived with my parents and my two siblings in a township called Mdantsane NU14. My father Robert was a self-employed taxi driver and my mother Notiti had various jobs, including working as a cleaning woman, a shoe saleswoman and boat designer. My parents separated when I was two years old. My older sister Zoleka was born in 1975 and my brother Xolisile was born in 1980. As time went by, I learned that I had other siblings from various affairs of my father's. If I've counted right, we're all in all ten children of different women. I am the youngest child of my parents.

My name is Thulani Tomose and I was born on 14 February 1984 in the city of East London in South Africa.

The dark side of my childhood

That's how the war started in my head. My father decided one day to throw my mother and her three children out of the house. That's how I got it from my mother, because I was just a two-year-old child when they split up. My mother went with me and my older brother and sister, Zoleka and Xolisile, to my maternal grandmother in the village of Kwelerha Nokhala. My grandmother was a wonderful woman. She would have given the shirt off her back to support my mother and us.

Mommy had to be unexpectedly alone with her three children without a husband, go back to the village and live there without getting any financial support from our father.

My mother is my idol. Strong and at the same time very sensitive, and a woman who I've never met the equal of in my 32 years of life. She's a unique woman, not because she's my mother, but because she's a woman I admire. Maybe she inherited her strength from my grandmother, who in 1962 had decided, after two unfortunate relationships, to raise her four children alone. She never wanted a man by her side again and she kept her word and was happy with her spiritual life. The years passed and my mother worked in the city as a cleaning lady with a light-skinned family in East London. At that time in South Africa dark-skinned and light-skinned were still extremely segregated. She was lucky to get a job with a family who was very nice to her. Later she got a better job at a water-skiing company called Kola-Ski and was very satisfied there.

My father came to my grandmother in the course of time and wanted to take me and my brother and sister to his house. But Mother refused to let him, agreeing that my father could only take us for the weekend. I was a little girl then and I don't remember it. There are two or three pictures of me as a kid that I got to see. My father decided not to return us to our mother, as discussed.

My mother finally took us away by the force and threat of my uncle Maboy. Since then my mother has forbidden me to deal with my father. She later met a new man: Markus. In the beginning it felt very strange with him, because we weren't used to seeing light-skinned men. The only light-skinned man was Mores, who ran our village shop.

Markus was the first light-skinned person whom I met at close range and got close to. I spoke no English at the time, only my mother tongue, Xhosa. Markus tried hard to learn our language and be able to express himself. He communicated well with us since he had learnt a little Xhosa from one of his employees in South Africa. Everybody was amazed with his wonderful nature. Markus and my mother were very much in love.

Markus originally came from Switzerland and had lived several years in South Africa. He already had a childless marriage behind him. He accepted us as his own children. Markus wanted to go back to Switzerland and take my mother with him. My mother refused to go with him at first, but my grandmother promised her she'd take good care of me and my siblings, as she had always done. So my mommy went to Switzerland in 1990, a few months before my sixth birthday. But she arranged for domestic help for my grandmother, who was ill. She got diabetes, thrombosis and old wounds and could not stand for long and run. The housemaid was older than my mother. We called her Qhini. That was her tribal name. The elderly loved to address someone with this name in my Xhosa tribal language.

Qhini was great to us and Grandma. She was very warm-hearted to all people. She was illiterate, as well as my grandmother and my mother, too.

Mommy and Markus came back after six months and brought so many great things with them. Dresses and, of course, sweets that we normally ate very rarely, because they were very expensive. It was wonderful seeing my mommy again and to have her with us. She took us to the beach 15 km away. It was a beautiful summer day. The whole family was together. We barbecued, listened to loud music and we kids danced. The grown-ups were drinking and talking and had fun as well as us kids did. Even as a child I loved dancing passionately. In the evening we drove together with different cars from Mommy's friends back to the village. Unfortunately, soon came the day Mommy and Markus went on vacation for four weeks and back to Switzerland. They got married there in 1990. There was no one present from Mommy's family or her friends, because we couldn't afford a trip to Switzerland.

Back then, no one from our family in the village had a telephone, so you could only make phone calls in the city in a public phone booth.

The city is located 15 km away from our village. Back then, no one in my family owned a car.

It was too expensive to take a taxi into town just to make a phone call. And so we only saw Mommy once a year in that time. Mommy had to pay for everything – for her own three children and my aunt Nokuku's five children, my mother's youngest sister. Of course, she also paid for our grandmother and Qhini and another cousin, Neli. Grandma only got a small pension, which my aunt Nozintombi helped herself to. She left almost nothing for my grandma.

My mother also sent money to support us. My aunt didn't give us any of it but she bought a bag of semolina and Amasi (natural yoghurt from fermented milk), Umngqusho, beans, a little sugar, oil and salt, and sent someone to bring it to us. Sometimes there were also chicken feet from the chickens she sold in the village. My grandmother sometimes earned a little money with her natural healing.

But the money was not enough and it also didn't come daily so that Grandmother could manage. In addition, she offered her services with passion, to help other people and not to make money, like she used to say to me. A little change or even just a thank you to my grandmother was perfectly sufficient.

Time passed and I was six years old. My birthday wasn't celebrated, but that wasn't bad for me. I was looking forward to school. When I went to the first class, I was not accompanied by an adult. Just my cousins who also lived with my grandmother and my brother and sister, who were already attending high school were by my side. I was very happy that day. The first day at school was great. We introduced ourselves and got instructions, which I, of course, couldn't keep as a whole. I was the youngest in my class, but I knew everyone from my village. I was dying to get close to my teacher's desk and watch everything she did. She let me sit next to her on the first day and said that this was an exception. The next day, I'd have to go back to my seat. It wasn't customary of her because she had a reputation at school and in the village for being very strict. At that time, teachers were allowed to use wooden sticks and hit the palms or fingertips of the students when they did not obey the teacher's instructions, were too late to school, didn't do their homework, were cheeky, did not participate hard enough in lessons, or the like.

The teachers were in charge at school. But also outside of the school, in the presence of teachers or other adults, one had to obey, whether you knew them or not.

Shortly before lunch, I slept at the table in front of my teacher. She let me sleep and my cousin fetched me and we went home to my grandmother. I told her everything and she and Qhini were happy with me.

I enjoyed school and I always had good grades. I was hard working and proud of my good grades. Grandmother praised us all and motivated us to continue in school, when we didn't feel like it anymore. She used to ask what we'd do with the money when we grow up. Sometimes I wanted to be a doctor, sometimes become a lawyer. She used to joke with us when we didn't feel like doing chores and said, we'd have to study hard and pay attention when at school to become what we wanted. That seemed pretty good to me because I wanted to be something when I was big, so I could help my family members and give back to them, as they didn't have much themselves. There was love and harmony with my grandmother and I felt comfortable, although sometimes I missed my mother. Then Mommy came back to visit us with her husband, Markus. My mother was happy and it was good to see her again and to have her with me. Unfortunately, this time they also left after four weeks, because they both had to work again.

One day, my cousin Lindeka and I were going home from school when a white station wagon stopped. Next to Am Tax sat my father. I recognized him, since he and I looked very much alike.

He said, "Molo Ntombam." (*Hello, my daughter*) He didn't get out of the car either, which was fine with me. I didn't know how to act. On the one hand, I was very happy to see my father, to talk to him for a moment, even though I knew that my grandmother and my aunt Nozintombi, who I also worked with and lived for a while, didn't approve of him.

I'd have to go, or I'd get in trouble if anyone found out. He gave me and my cousin Lindeka two rand each. Back then it was a lot of pocket money if you didn't have your own. He wanted to give us a lift in his taxi, but I turned him down because I was afraid that we might get seen by someone. So he went on in his station wagon and we walked to Grandma's house. When we arrived, we told her and she wasn't thrilled. My grandmother told me again that she didn't want me to go out with my dad.

I talked to him on the street once. She also asked me not to take anything else from him. I was sad and I didn't understand it.

Of course I didn't let my grandmother see that since I was afraid of her reaction. I was disappointed because I was hoping for something when I told her about my encounter with my father. I was trying to understand what kind of problem they had with my father, because no one explained it to me. They only said that I shouldn't talk to him. After all, we were allowed to keep the money we took from my father, and we were allowed to buy with it what we wanted. There was candy for everyone and everything was fine again. My dad used to take his combi-taxi to our house from time to time to drop off passengers. I saw his cab sometimes while I was out playing and it made me sad that I couldn't talk to him, but I didn't let anyone know I cared.

All I ever heard was bad things about my father but I couldn't see it myself. I wished so badly that I could talk to him.

One day I was walking through the woods with my cousin Lindeka.

Lindeka was like my sister; we liked each other and were the same age. Again my father drove beside us and spoke to us. He greeted us and acted very friendly as always. My heart opened and I was very happy to see him, but I also knew I wasn't supposed to talk to him. I told him that he shouldn't talk to me again in the future because otherwise I'd really get in trouble. He still gave us a pack of bananas and a pack of apples. I took it, thanked him and hugged him. I gave him a kiss and he kissed me goodbye for the last time. At least, I thought so.

My feelings fluctuated between joy and fear of my grandmother and especially in front of my Aunt Nozintombi and their reaction when they found out that I had talked to my father and accepted the fruit. So we went home and I told my grandmother about it and who gave me the fruit. She was very upset and threatened to beat the crap out of me the next time I took something from him. I was even sadder than the last time and cried secretly. Nobody noticed, and I pretended nothing happened.

A week went by. Then I saw his combi-taxi on the road again and ran away from him. He had noticed me and shouted my name. But I didn't react and neither looked back. It went like that a few more times, until I didn't see him any more in our village.

Time passed. My grandmother became very ill and had to be taken to the hospital. She was in a diabetic coma for three months and had to stay in the hospital. My sister and I had to go and stay at my Aunt Nozintombi's. My brother went to my father but ran away from him and came to my aunt, back to the village. My aunt was very strict and scolded me a lot and I was afraid of her, but we had to stay with her. I got used to it quickly and it wasn't that bad, I thought, living with her.

When my sister was 18 years old, she was in love with a neighbor boy and he was in love with her. They wanted to see each other, but no one should know except for me and my cousins, Aphiwe and Neli. We had a secret word for it-Unquntsuza. We used it when the couple was sneaking out or in during the night.

Then, I quietly opened the door for them. My cousin didn't notice and her parents – my aunt and uncle – didn't squeal. She knew I could keep a secret, so she confided in me. My sister had one night overslept with him the next day and missed school the day after. Of course, my aunt noticed, because in the morning she wasn't home. When my sister finally got home, she tried to find an excuse why she hadn't gone to school. Unfortunately, my aunt had seen my sister from the house of Sicelo, her boyfriend from the neighboring house and how they kissed. She already had impatiently waited for my sister's arrival and left without asking with the stick in her hand. We couldn't warn her. My aunt waited for her at the door . She hit her for so long that she had to be taken to the hospital for her wounds to be treated. My sister went to my father in the end and finished her last year of school in the village.

My father drove them daily to the school of the village Mdantsane and picked her up again. My sister still didn't come to my aunt to visit us, even though her school was not a long way from us. My aunt told me that my sister had decided to live with my father, that this was her will.

I was sad to hear she wasn't to live with us anymore but I understood her. One day I was in bed, asleep. The room was so dark you couldn't see anything. I slept in a double bed with my two cousins, Aphiwe, the first daughter of my aunt Nozintombi, and Lindeka, the daughter of my other aunt, Nokuku. Both slept in one direction and me in the other one. I slept in a worn out dress because I didn't have pyjamas. I was ripped out of a deep sleep when I felt a cold hand gently caressing my buttocks. I thought nothing of it at the moment, turned a bit and quickly fell asleep again.

The next night, I felt that caress again on my buttocks. I turned around and I could see someone who hadn't been there when I went to bed.

It was my cousin Songezo. I just slipped away and then he went back to his own room and fell asleep again. At that time I was already eight years old. I awoke again when that same night I felt Songezo, who was two years older than me, with his penis on my buttocks. He moved back and forth. I knew it wasn't okay and his penis shouldn't be there. I lay frozen on the edge of the bed and did not move. I was paralyzed. He had, while I was asleep, pushed up my dress and my underpants a little bit without me even noticing. I still heard his breath behind me and felt him rubbing against me faster and faster. Suddenly he stopped and I felt something wet and warm dripping on my buttock cleft. I was still motionless and said nothing. I felt him get up very carefully and leave the room sneakily. I cautiously touched something wet. It was a disgusting, slimy fluid running down my buttock cleft to my vagina. I didn't know it was sperm at the time, because I wasn't enlightened by anyone, but I knew that his penis didn't belong near my genitals and cleft buttocks.

I couldn't fall asleep again and cried silently until morning, when everyone got up as usual. I was the only one with swollen eyes this morning. I was ashamed of myself. My cousin Lindeka asked me if everything was all right.

"Why do you have swollen eyes and you're so weird?" she asked me.

I said it was all right, I just had a bad night's sleep last night. My cousin was present and he pretended as if nothing had happened and even sought my eye contact, but I couldn't return it. I was disgusted with him. That's when I missed my grandmother the most. Only she could have helped me. I developed a hatred for Songezo like I'd never known before.

What bothered me the most was that he pretended nothing had happened. He laughed and was content and normal as always. I was devastated internally and thought only: My cousin? That can't be!

I was thinking a lot that day, but I dared not to tell anyone what he'd done. I was thinking if I didn't tell anyone, I'd forget it someday. But I'm afraid that wasn't the case. It kept me busy, and I talked with no one about it. Not even with Lindeka, whom I most trusted. That same night, I asked Lindeka to lie in the same direction with me. She looked at me and asked what was different today? I said I felt better when she was next to me, because last night I had this bad dream.

She laughed and agreed. Nothing happened that night. I also stayed awake consciously for a long time and listened to see whether he would come again. My aunt and uncle slept together. in a different house than we kids. I went through a lot of my secret to tell.

There was a lot on my mind and I cried, afraid that my cousin would come back as soon as I fell asleep. Nothing happened for weeks and I thought it was over. One night I woke up because I felt something on my genitals. It was my cousin's hand. He had already pulled up my dress and pulled down my underpants. He grasped my vagina and fingered it. At the same time, he rubbed his penis on my buttock cleft and breathed on my ear. He tried not to breathe loudly, but he was so close to my ear I heard every breath he gave me. It disgusted me. I said and did nothing out of fear. My cousin thought I was sleeping.

The next day, it all seemed like a dream, because my cousin behaved perfectly normally. He laughed and cracked jokes and pretended there was nothing and this hate in me grew more and more that I couldn't stand against it and fight him off. I knew no one would believe me if I did that. After all, my cousin was the son of my aunt and my uncle and they would stick by him. By saying something, I'd only make it worse for myself. So I kept quiet.

But my nightmare didn't end. The next day I decided I'd never sleep in a dress again. I'd only sleep in pants. Well I'd definitely notice when he tried to undress me, I thought, but I was wrong. I got tired and fell asleep at some point. I only noticed him when he tried to put his fingers in my vagina. I was shocked and I kept shifting in bed. I wanted him to realize that I was awake and didn't want what he did to me. He stayed calm and my heart pounded like crazy. He pulled his hand back and left the bed silently. I couldn't hold back my tears. On the one hand, I was relieved that he was gone, but on the other hand, I was afraid that he might come back later. The next day, as usual, he was normal. I went with my cousin Lindeka to school. I wish I'd told her my secret, but I couldn't. I felt such mixed feelings as despair, anger, shame, but I decided to keep it to myself. My aunt lived 15 to 20 minutes walk from the school. We always walked. At the time, I had two best friends of the same age, whom I liked very much: Nonkosi and Andiswa. We used to walk to school together every morning and shared everything, but I didn't share that secret with them. I tried as hard as I could to make sure that no one knew, laughing and trying to look happy.

From then on, almost every night went like this: trying not to fall asleep and keeping watch.

Of course I was tired during the day and slept sometimes while I put Zintle, my little cousin, to bed. My cousin didn't come even when I was awake. After a while nothing happened anymore and I was able to get back to my normal sleep.

My aunt asked me one night to keep an eye on my cousin Zintle because the girl was very attached to me. I was very happy to do it, too. My aunt and my uncle wanted to work on a special event in the nearby church. I was glad I didn't have to go. I am very ecclesiastical, though, and believe in God, but it always bored me to go to church.

I had to go to mass, because my aunt and my uncle made me go every Sunday. My aunt always told me Zintle was like my baby, because she only wanted to be fed and diapered by me. She always wanted to sleep with me and I brought her first, when she was asleep, to my aunt's bed so that she would think she fell asleep with me. Then my aunt went off. I bathed the little one, put lotion on her and put her pyjamas on. Then I fed her with vegetable porridge and warm milk. She loved to sit on my back wrapped in a towel. She fell fast asleep when I was doing the dishes. Then I put the girl to bed. Suddenly, there was a knock on the door. It was already dark in the village. Since there wasn't any electricity, it was dark in the streets and you either used candles or camping and paraffin lamps.

My aunt told me I was supposed to open the door only for family members. I shouldn't open it to anyone else. I asked who was there. A male voice answered. It was a cousin, the son of my aunt and mommy's cousin. He was here in Kwelerha for his circumcision. Every now and then he stopped by my aunt's to visit her while he was in the village.

I didn't know him that well, because it was the first time he'd ever been at this traditional time with us in the village. Circumcision was a fixed ritual in the everyday life of my Xhosa tribe. You're only a man if you've endured circumcision in the bush. A bushman performs the circumcision with his special knife and the wounds are disinfected and cured using nature's leaves, without the need for a doctor or medication. This is required unless you're in danger of death, but then you've failed the test as a man. The women build a temporary house from hay and the married women and the young women who already have their periods stay in it until the ritual in the bushes is complete. I was still allowed to go, because I did not have a period yet, but sometimes we took the food to Abakhwetha. That's what we called my cousin during this month in the bush. During this time, you can't use the man's real name. They have to live in the forest for about a month.

They don't come home in that time, or they are despised and not considered to be men. If they survive this time, there will be a great feast for them and they may go back home to be received as men. I opened the door, and since I was younger, I couldn't call him by his name. We in the Xhosa tribe called the men Bhuti and the women Sisi out of respect.

I greeted him. He sat down. I asked him if he had eaten. He said he just wanted a glass of water. I went into the kitchen and got it. He sat on the larger of the two sofas and I took the other seat opposite. I asked him if he had a message for my aunt because he didn't say anything. He asked where she and the rest of the family were right now and why I was alone. He asked me if I wasn't afraid being alone.

I said, "No, Zintle's asleep, and the others will be back soon." You could even hear them singing there. "They'll be back by 10:00," I told him. He looked at his watch and said, "Well, you won't be alone much longer. It's already 8:30 p. m. and you're already tall."

I said, smiling, "Yes, but it's nice to have someone here." He got up. He was a very big man and very well built. His face was painted with the chalk typical for this traditional time. Once they'd gone through the ritual and become real men, they also had to completely dress themselves anew.

I asked him if he wanted to go. My aunt would come home any moment now. All he said was, "I know," and he made a dirty grin. Then he sat next to me. I wanted to get up again because I was getting scared, but he took my hand, pushed me down and ordered me to stay seated with a raw voice. I was very afraid and wondered why he was like that all of a sudden. I told him that I was tired and wanted to go to sleep, hoping he'd leave then. But instead, he pushed me down into a lying position.

I started screaming that he should let me go, but he didn't. He grabbed my neck when I started screaming, so I couldn't breathe, and then he let go again and said, "Stay calm and you'll get no harm."

I tried to defend myself, but it was hopeless. He pulled down my pants and unzipped his zipper. I panicked and sweated. He looked at me with his cold eyes. I felt tears running down my face. Then he pushed me into one corner of the sofa. I fought no more, because I was hoping he wouldn't hurt me then.

He wouldn't stop, though. He held me even tighter. As he realized I was doing nothing but crying, he started to grope all over the place. His hands were everywhere, anywhere they shouldn't be. He stuck his fingers in my vagina first. I didn't move anymore and it hurt like hell. When he came up to me with his giant penis and tried to push himself in, I tried to squeeze my legs together. But I didn't stand a chance against him. I cried, scratched him, tried to bite him. Then he became even more aggressive. Against such a great and strong man I was completely powerless. He stuck his giant penis into my vagina, and it hurt like a knife had been rammed between my legs. I thought at that moment I was going to die. I was hoping just somebody would come into the room and save me. I cried and it all hurt me. I felt so powerless, disgusting, dirty. I waited in vain for some- one to come, and he went on. That's how I lost my virginity.

When he was done, he dressed again, as if nothing had hap- pened. He looked at his watch and said if anyone found out, he'd hurt me even more. Besides, who would believe me yet? He'd still be three weeks in the village.

He was very aggressive while he was saying that. I assured him with teary eyes and a trembling voice that I had understood. He told me to wash up and if anyone noticed anything, he'd make me feel it.

With trembling knees I made an effort to get up. Liquid mixed with blood was running out of my sheath and dripping onto the floor. He only commented on this, instructing me to hurry and wipe the dirt off the floor. I went to wash myself.

I was still bleeding, everything in me was burning and I could barely walk. He ordered me, again, to walk normally when I finished washing up and went back to the living room. I sat down and couldn't look him in the eyes. I felt such a sense of disgust and wished that he would leave, but he remained seated, as if nothing had happened. I heard the voices. They were coming from the window under which I was sitting.

I pretended to be falling asleep on the sofa so that no one could see that I was crying. Everyone came back from the church. My aunt said to my rapist, "Take her to bed."

She thought I had fallen asleep. I quickly said that I'd woken up and would go to bed myself. I asked my aunt if I could sleep in the house with her. I was hoping for a yes because I was scared. But she said we had our own bed at the Ronta house, where all the children slept. I said okay.

She asked what was wrong with my eyes. I said I fell asleep and I was very tired but I would go to bed now. We finally all went to the Ronta house. My rapist stayed in the house with my aunt and uncle. Aphiwe and Neli told me our secret word when they wanted to leave: Unquntsuza. I stayed in bed. When Songezo and Akhona fell asleep quietly, I locked the door from the inside. We had a deal to throw a little rock at the window to get back in. They left and I started to realize everything that had happened today.

I cried and asked myself: Why? One day I fell asleep. I awoke when I thought my nightmare was over.

There was Songezo again, rubbing my cleft buttocks and my vagina with his penis. I remained like dead, didn't move and didn't say anything. When he was done, he went back to his bed.

I stayed awake and I saw it all over again. During sleep there was nothing to think of anymore. When the two of them got home early in the morning, I was still wide awake. I opened the door for them and they sneaked into bed. The next day I couldn't be alone with Songezo in one room. But I had decided not to say anything to anybody. As always, he pretended nothing had happened.

Luckily, the other cousin didn't live with us and soon left because he didn't usually live in Kwelerha. He came to his last day to say goodbye to my aunt and to thank her. Our looks hardly ever met, I couldn't look him in the eye any more than I could Songezo. I felt a sense of disgust when I saw him, and I didn't know if those feelings would ever go away.

That was my everyday life with my aunt. I couldn't share my secret with anyone. One day, my mother told me that my father was in the village and she allowed me to go for a ride with him. I was so excited and had a great time.

I was afraid of my aunt at the same time. 'Cause my aunt wasn't like my grandmother, who only warned me. My aunt hit me immediately.

She beat me a lot because I was a long-time bed-wetter and she didn't like it at all. But I didn't think long and ran outside, where my dad was already in his white cab. I had a station wagon waiting for me. I was happy to see my father. He hadn't been in our village for a while. My father was smiling at me and was happy to see me, too. He told me to get in. We'd go for a ride around our village.

I was sitting next to my father and it was so good. But I didn't feel like trusting him with my secret. Suddenly my worry was blown away. I felt like I was protected and safe next to him. My dad told me we were going to Xoli's school, too. Xoli was my brother's nickname. My father said that I should duck down at my brother's school, so no one could see me and I couldn't get in trouble with my aunt.

I did as he said. When we arrived, I could sit up again. My father got out with me and said I should wait by the car while he got Xoli out of class. The teacher let it happen. My father explained to us that he would take us into town and bring us back later before school finished so that my aunt wouldn't know.

He drove off. He didn't ask us; he just did it. My brother said nothing. He seemed depressed to me, not enthusiastic about our father's idea. But I was just happy, and I didn't want to be involved with the consequences. I wanted to get to grips with it first. But instead of going into town, my dad passed it. My brother asked where we were going.

My father told us we were going to his house. Xoli didn't say another word. Then we arrived at his place. We were warmly welcomed by Nozimbo, my father's wife, as well as by her own four sons from an earlier marriage and their daughter with my father. My older sister Zoleka was there, too. I was so happy and she was also very happy to see us. There were several more children. I knew only my Sister Zoleka and Xoli, I didn't know the rest.

The eldest son of Nozimbo is called Themba (1974), the daughter Anathi (1978), his second son Thabo (1980).There was also their niece, Akhona, (1982), and three more sons of my father from different women: Munda (1978), Bangile (1982) and Thembekile (1979).

Everyone introduced themselves and my father told me that these were all our brothers and sisters. I didn't know at the time that the four children weren't my biological father's.

It was already getting dark outside and my dad hadn't done anything to get us back to the village. So I asked when we would return, because our aunt would surely be worried about us. We would also be in trouble if we didn't leave soon. I also asked him to go back with us and to explain to our aunt where we'd been for so long. But my father just said, "You're staying here now."

I didn't understand what he meant by that, so I asked. He replied that he had decided to take us to his house and he hadn't wanted to tell us that in the village. He meant that he'd already talked to the schools for us and tomorrow we'd be at the head offices of our new schools.

I wasn't too excited about the idea of being able to go to a hospital to live with him. On the other hand, I liked the situation at my aunt's no better. I kept quiet and left the room where he and his wife Nozimbo had retired. I felt lost and was confused by the situation. My longing for my grandmother grew. I was sad, but I was used to not showing my feelings. So my father had the last word. He had it all split up, who slept where. So I got my first place to sleep on the floor with some old blankets and a straw mat.

I didn't mind sleeping on the floor. I just thought that it was better than what my cousin Songezo and the other one had done to me. The first night was over. My father and his wife went to my new school with me. That was new to me and I liked it. I didn't think much of my aunt and what she would think. Since I was good at school, I didn't have any problems with the changeover. I got into second grade in the middle of the year.

I was in the same class with my half-brother, Bangile. I was glad to see at least one familiar face.

He was my brother, but I'd only known him for a day. Akhona and Lwazi went to the same school as me, too, a class before me, and my brother Xoli went to high school and that's why we didn't go to the same school. I went to Siyanda School, and he got into the Shedrack school and Thabo also went to the same school with Xoli. The first day of school lasted until 2 p.m. and we got from my dad a rand for lunch, because we couldn't go home at noon, as it was too far.

When school was over, I ran back with Akhona. We got along great from the first day on and we slept under a blanket, too. When we got home, my stepmother was still in bed and she ordered us to clean the whole house. She told me I had to cook for the whole family, too. I was almost nine years old at the time and did not disagree.

She also told me from now on she would be my mother and the only one. From now on, I should call her Mama. That I did, too. It was funny, but I did it. My father was on the road a lot at that time as an independent taxi driver. When we were done with the house, I wanted to play with the neighbor's kids. So I asked Akhona if we could go and play. Her answer was no. We were not allowed to have friends and play with them.

I was shocked and sad and didn't understand. For me it was customary after school, after I had fulfilled my duties, to play. My stepmother called me and asked if I had washed my school shirt for she wouldn't be my babysitter.

I asked her for soap. She replied that I had to buy the soap myself with my own money. I said I didn't have any money. Then she just said that I had to be careful, starting tomorrow, not to use up everything at school. I didn't understand it, because that one rand was not enough even for lunch.

In the evening, my father came back home. I was so happy when he was back. I asked my father if he could buy me buy some soap. He asked me if I'd used up all the soap he'd bought. His wife replied, "Yes, it's been used up."

He gave her money so she could buy us new soap. The next morning, we had to leave Nozimbo in front of the school and my dad had given her the money for lunch, too.

She was lying in bed as usual when Akhona and I went to her. Everybody got the money but me. I asked if I could get the money. She said that there was not any for me today. I should make myself scarce. And if I had something to say to my father, I'd get what I deserved. She was mad at me. So I went to school and didn't say anything. Akhona shared her lunch with me on that day and asked me not to say anything, otherwise she would not get any money next time, either. I promised her. But I was very sad. Later on I cried alone in the toilets. I had also lost the desire to play. After school, we returned home. My stepmother was still in bed when we got out of school around 3:00. The first thing she asked me to do for her was to boil water and pour it into a sink and soap her laundry and cloths. I did the work as she wanted it, because I didn't want anything else to go wrong that day. She seemed satisfied and told me that to make her bed, wipe the room and dust it off while she washed herself. I did everything, because I was used to cleaning and babysitting, but I still couldn't cook alone for so many people.

When she was done, I was supposed to clean it all up, and she also said next time I would have to put things away. She didn't want to have to call me again. I should estimate when she'd be done washing. She also told me that I had her room super cleaned. I was very happy to hear that. She gave me money to buy Slice — white bread — and four or five loaves of brown bread and four to five packages of Drink Pop. It's like something like syrup. Also, a box of six eggs and a bottle. I should also bring Coca Cola and oil with me – and yes, hurry.

The shop was five to ten minutes walk from home. I went and on the way back I saw our neighbor, Noziyeye, who could barely carry her groceries. I offered to help her. She looked at me for a long time and smiled, then took me and held me tightly in her arms. I was surprised that she was so happy to see me. She stopped and started telling me that she had been good friends with my mother. That she had been present when I was born and had been with me until the age of two, and hadn't seen me since. She pressed me and tears of joy ran down her face. I was happy, too. She seemed so nice. I forgot Nozimbo's instructions that I should hurry. But the closer we got, the more scared I became. I helped our neighbor with her groceries all the way to the door. She pushed me again and asked me to wait a minute. She gave me two rand and thanked me. I turned down the money and told her I was happy to do it. But she wouldn't let me go. So I took the money and went home. When I arrived, my stepmother was already at the door waiting for me. I'll never forget her look.

All she said was, "Put the bags on the table and come with me in my room." I went with her and thought she'd yell at me right now. Being frightened, I started telling stories: I was in a hurry. On the way back the neighbor needed help.

My grandmother had always told me that I should help people, especially older ones, who should be treated with special respect. I also told her that the neighbor had given me two rands. "Give me the money," demanded my stepmother. I gave it without hesitation. Then she closed the door of her room, opened her wardrobe, pulled out a belt of my father's, and hit me.

I screamed because it hurt so much while I was trying to protect my face. She yelled at me saying that I should never talk with that prostitute about my mother again. One that had gone away with a white man.

When she had yelled enough, she ordered me to dry my tears and to give her the eggs and all the white bread and the Coke.

"You cut the brown bread into quarters and make them sweetaid (a kind of syrup) and give it to the others so that they can eat
and drink. And when you're done you can the brown bread and
sweetaid. " I prepared her eggs the way she liked them: fried with
flavouring. Making eggs wasn't a problem for me. That wasn't
difficult. I brought her the fried six eggs and thought she'd at least
give me one of them, but that wasn't the case. She ate exactly one
egg and she gave the rest to Thabo, Lwando and Lwazi. They
were allowed in their room behind closed doors drinking cola and
then coming back with empty plates and empty two-liter bottles.
I was sick and my longing for my grandmother grew immeasur-
ably. While I was out washing my school clothes, tears ran down
my face. My stepmother watched me from her bedroom window.
She called my name and I trembled with fear. On my way into
the house I wiped the tears from my eyes. She asked me why I
was crying. I didn't say anything. She closed the door again and
took the belt out and hit me. But I still didn't tell her why I had
been crying. She told me she was gonna hit me until I told her.

I didn't do it. She stopped at some point and I felt the blows
no more. "Get out of my sight," my stepmother finally ordered.
I went and washed my laundry. In the evening, my sister and
father came from work. My sister still went to Jongilanga High
School and travelled with my dad every morning since he had
customers in the village. And after school, she was with my father until the end of the working day when they would return
home together.

What we didn't know at that time was that my mother from
Switzerland supported my sister completely financially. My mother also told my father that she wanted my sister to go to a city
school and after that to study to be a vet. She should be what she
wanted to be. But my father preferred to put the money in his
own pocket and was with my sister after school from Monday
to Friday until 10 to 11 at night.

The next day she had to get up again at 5 o'clock. My sister
also had to prepare water for her bath. Every morning, she had
to boil water. We – my sister, Akhona, Anathi and me -should
get his clothes ready taking turns in the evening. Previously, the

appropriate clothes should be selected and ironed wrinkle-free. Even his shoes had to be polished and be ready. Both of them didn't realize what was happening here in everyday life. She sent us to bed early, although there was no fixed bedtime. I went to bed speechless that night. I could neither cry nor sleep. I was pretending. I waited until I knew that my father was in his room, too. I wanted to see my sister. She looked at me because I had swollen eyes. I get big eyes when I cry and she knew that. My sister asked quietly what had happened. "Mama (my stepmother) hit me." She asked me why, and I told her everything. My sister couldn't eat that night. She seemed stressed after I told her everything. I panicked, fearing she'd betray me. But, surprisingly, she didn't seem to be okay with what her mom had done.

At least that night I felt a little understood and fell asleep. I'd been there a week now. It was Thursday, when we got out of school and my stepmother was in a hurry. She very rarely left her bed and the house even rarer. I was glad she wanted to go out. A little distance from her was good for me, because I had very mixed feelings about her. It was a mixture of hate, anger and fear. She told us she had to leave for two hours and didn't say where she was going. She gave us instructions on what to do in her absence and set off on her way. My brother unlocked the gate, which looked like a prison gate, and gave her the key.

She took the key with her. My stepmother allowed the boys to go out with the other boys and play in the neighborhood. But Akhona and I were not allowed to leave the farm. We were only allowed in the courtyard. We weren't allowed in the living room on the sofa, either, to sit and watch TV. Thabo, the son of my stepmother, came up with the idea, and despite TV grounding, he was zapping through the programs and sitting on the sofa. Akhona and I were afraid to join and did our duty, even though I would have loved to watch TV. Because with Grandma we hadn't had that chance. Xoli had also transferred tasks from our stepmother to us, that he conscientiously took care of. He cooked semolina and bones for the dogs and fed it to them.

When Akhona and I were done with the household, we suddenly heard loud screams from the living room. It was my stepmother's youngest son, Lwazi. We hurried to him and we saw Thabo standing in front of the TV, which didn't work anymore. He had something which he couldn't take back. Panic rose in him. He called on Xoli for help, as he was very skillful in dealing with electronic stuff. I've never seen anything like this electronic before. Xoli tried and tried and the snow-white picture became just a black and nothing worked anymore. At the very moment Xoli was still trying to solve the problem, my stepmother came into the living room. We were all paralyzed, because we had miscalculated her return.

She didn't ask what had happened. She went after Xoli and dragged him by the collar of his T-shirt from the living room into her bedroom and closed the door behind her. We heard yelling from outside and could not see anything. We heard Xoli a short time after and then the strikes.

Every beat hurt my heart. I would have liked to see the beating for he had done nothing. My brother was much more afraid of being beaten as a child than I was. Thabo laughed and didn't confess that he had turned on the TV and broken it.

She beat Xoli and strangled him until he urinated; only then did she let him go. I could hear every word and every blow, since the walls were very thin. He said several times that he was sorry, and he asked her not to kill him. My brother came out of the bedroom crying and ran out of the house. I stood there with tears running down my face, afraid she'd kill him. She saw me and started yelling at me why I was useless and if I had nothing better to do. I apologized and left the house, too. I couldn't comfort my brother, because I didn't want my stepmother to see. She kept us at a distance. That same night, when my father came home, my brother was already in bed and asleep. My father's wife came to me in her dressing gown. She pointed to the broken TV and told me it was Xoli.

My father didn't ask any questions. He just walked out of the house, got a plastic pipe and hit my sleeping brother. His wife didn't tell him that she had already brutally hit him in the first place. My brother fled the house. My father was furious and ordered Thabo, Lwando, Bangile and Lwazi to stop him and bring him back. Xoli should learn his lesson.

I suddenly recognized a monster in the facial features of my father and thought of how my grandmother and my aunt had warned me not to talk to him. There was so much going through my mind at that moment. I blamed myself that we had landed here because my brother had kept no contact with him on the street like I had done in the village. My longing for my old life was at this moment growing bigger and bigger, even when I was thinking of my cousin Songezo and what he had done to me. It felt less bad than what we suffered at the moment.

I didn't recognize our dear father. I was afraid for my brother. I thought my father would kill him. The boys came back without Xoli. They hadn't found him. For a brief moment, a stone fell from my heart and I was glad they couldn't catch him. But, then, I wondered if anything might have happened to him. I could never have forgiven myself for that. My father went on his way and searched in his car where he suspected my brother was, with Uncle Maboy. My uncle Maboy, my mother's brother, lived at the time in Mdantsane, too. My brother had actually gone into hiding with him. Uncle offered him a place to sleep in his nursery with the other cousins of ours. My brother later told me that he had heard the voice of our father when he asked my uncle if Xoli was there.

My uncle wasn't very fond of my father, either. That's why I was never allowed to never visit my cousins or talk with them, and this made me sad. They lived just ten minutes' walk from us. Sometimes I'd see my cousin Thabisa, who was the same age I was, running past me with her friends and she waved at me from afar every time as she knew that I was not allowed to talk to her. My brother also told me that he panicked when he heard my father at the door, climbed out of the window and ran away from there barefoot.

In my father's car, the four boys sat and waited for him when they saw Xoli climbing out of the window. They immediately shouted out to my father, "There's Xoli!" My dad and my uncle looked around for Xoli but were unsuccessful at finding him. Eventually they came back without him. That night, I could barely sleep. I was plagued by guilt and the fear that something might happen to my brother. I cried secretly while everyone was asleep. My sister was plagued by migraine. Knowing my sister well, I knew that she was stressed and that's why she'd gotten this severe headache.

I'd have liked to have shared my worries with her. It wasn't possible because we all slept in the same room and could not talk about Xoli without being heard by the others. So each one of us stayed alone with her worries.

My father went to work as usual and took my Sister Zoleka with him. The day after went on as usual, as if nothing had happened. No one spoke of the previous evening and no one tried to find Xoli again. Akhona and I went into the bedroom to say goodbye and get our one rand for lunch, then we were on our way to school. That morning I was calmer than usual. Akhona noticed that of course and tried to make me laugh. I told her I wasn't well and I had a headache.

That wasn't true, of course. I confided in her a few things, but not everything, because I was afraid that she would betray me. But I didn't want any more trouble and figured out how to make everything perfect. It was lunch break. I walked into the schoolyard alone.

I wanted to let my feelings run wild. At the same moment, Nahmla, my only trusted school friend, came to me. She knew what was going on at my house. She had a story similar to mine with her stepmother. Her mother had lost her way too soon. Namhla knew many things no one else knew. I knew her secrets and she knew mine. I trusted her very much, but not with the abuse story of my cousins. Namhla came to me and told me that my brother was looking for me and where he'd been hiding. She took me to his hideout. I will never be able to forget this image of seeing my brother. He had wrapped himself in a plastic bag so he could protect himself from the cold. He was barefoot. His lips were dried out and had cracks. He'd had no food or drink for a day. He told me he would have slept on the water channel. Xoli tried to fool me. I knew him well – he never wanted anyone to get hurt because of him. I was sad. And he was trying to convince me that he was fine. He told me he'd only come for a moment to see me and that he had decided to go back to the village. I tried everything I could to change his mind, because I was worried sick for him. Besides, I felt a lot of guilt. I cried and promised him I'd talk to our father and I also told him he'd certainly calmed down.

I didn't know that, of course. I just didn't want anything to happen to him. My brother promised me he'd go home tonight and come and talk to our father and our stepmother and apologize. He hugged me, gave me a kiss and left. It had been customary for my grandmother at the time to kiss each other on the mouth and to hug each other farewell. My father was ruled by different rules, and I never hugged him again. In his household there was no love. I was sad and at the same time I was happy about the end of the school year and, most of all, the evening when my brother would come home again.

My break was over and Namhla was waiting for me. I didn't have to tell her everything. Namhla was a very sensitive young woman. She asked me if I was okay anyway. I smiled and said, "Yes, I'm fine, Namhla, really." We then went to class and were looking forward to the end of the school year. Then it was finally time. I ran home. I decided not to tell anyone that I knew of Xoli and that he was coming home tonight. I was pleased, but at the same time I was afraid for my brother. Would they hit him again because he'd run away? Joy quickly gave way to the sad reality and worry. It was already dark and still no sign of my brother. Deep in my sorrows, I suddenly heard the honking horn of my dad's car. That was his sign that one of the boys should unlock the gate for him. My father and sister Zoleka finally came in and I had the hope that my brother had just been waiting to come into the house. It was already late, about 9 pm.

After my father had freshened up and then had his dinner, I was so excited and every time there was a knock on the door, I hoped all the more that it could be my brother. When my sister went to the kitchen after dinner, I followed her secretly and whispered that I had met Xoli and he had told me he was coming back tonight. She was relieved and asked very quickly: "Today?" I said yes. Then she said to me, "Well, go back to the room and keep it to yourself. Not that you get in trouble because you have not said anything." When our lascivious conversation was over, I did as she had advised me, and went from the kitchen in the direction of our children's room, where we all stayed.

Meanwhile, my father called me. That was one of many rules here, too. You always had to be mindful and listen when called upon, because my father and my stepmother didn't want to have to call twice otherwise there was trouble. On good days you were insulted and on a bad day you'd be beaten with a belt. So the next time you could hear better was the reason they gave. I was glad that he called my name, because I knew he had kept a bit of his dinner and sweet drinks like Coca Cola or Fanta for me. My stepmother and my father ate and drank different things from us kids. He told me to sit down and eat the rest. And my stepmother watched critically. If looks could kill, it would have happened at that moment. I did as my father had commanded me, looked at the ground and ate the little thing he had left. There was some chicken and some Coca Cola left and I ate everything . From my grandmother and my mother I had been brought up differently. I should always share everything, no matter how much or how little it was. That's why I had a guilty conscience now.

I didn't get anything for the kids. When I was done, I brought the dishes into the kitchen. After I washed everything off, I had to go back to my father. I went back to his bedroom, and he told me to go to the bathroom. I was supposed to stroke his feet until he fell asleep. So I stroked his feet and feared inwardly that he would fall asleep before Xoli came. However, my father was tired and fell asleep quickly. I sneaked out and had the hope that Xoli would still be able to come, as he had promised me. Most of my siblings were asleep. My sister and I waited full of hope and were not able to share our thoughts. I was worried and afraid for him. I was like my sister. It was a long Friday night for me, because I couldn't fall asleep as I was so worried. My thoughts that night circled around my brother.

Saturday morning came. My father stayed at home. He usually worked Saturday, but today he wanted to fix something on the car. No one spoke of Xoli that day. Everybody had their hands full with their own duties. Mine was cooking today. For the first time. Cooking complete dinners. I had cooked several times but never more complex dishes. My sister Zoleka should introduce me to them. My sister was a great cook. She first showed me how to cook rice. She helped me and wasn't just standing there. My sister showed me exactly what to do and was very patient.

I did everything the way she told me to. We cut vegetables, butter, nuts and chicken, and she showed me everything with a lot of patience. Everything, step by step. In the end she was very proud and said to me, "Look at your work!" I was so happy that I had prepared a real meal for so many people. But I was glad I didn't have to do it every day, because cooking for so many people still wasn't that easy for me. I was afraid that the next time I would have to do it on my own. My stepmother had made it very clear to me that next time I'd have to cook alone without the help of my sister.

I then went outside to get my father and saw my aunt Nozintombi and two men I didn't know. I was very happy to see my aunt. She was behind closed doors at my father's yard. I stopped and didn't know how to react. I was waiting for my father's reaction. He spoke while he stood there with my aunt and the gentlemen. I couldn't understand every word and my sister was already calling out to me. I pretended I didn't hear her because I was waiting for the reaction of my father. My sister came to me and asked what I was waiting for. The water that we always prepared for our father to wash would get cold. I said Father was talking to Aunt Nozintombi.

My sister went to them and asked me to wait. I did as she said, but I was very nervous. At the same moment, my stepmother came to me and asked if I had anything to do. I said yes, and she asked why I was standing there. I told her I was gonna call Dad to wash but he was still speaking.

She told me to go inside the house. When I went in, I heard my aunt scream. Then my sister came into the house. Behind her was my stepmother. She told me that I should put aside her and my father's food and went out again. My sister gave me instructions to count them all, so I wouldn't forget anyone while I was handing out the food. Then I wouldn't get dinner. Since we didn't have a microwave and so we could not warm up the food later, my sister ordered me to fill two pots of boiling water and place the plates there for my father and my stepmother so that the food would stay warm. My sister didn't say a word about what was going on outside and I realized she was trying to distract me. When my look fell out of the window, she told me immediately: "Concentrate!"

I obeyed and began to serve the food. First the adults and then the children by age. When I was done, I sat down on the floor of the hall. The adults were sitting in the kitchen at the table. Only the adults were allowed to sit at the dining table and we kids sat on the floor. My father and my stepmother finally came out of the house after the long interlude. My father just said I could bring the water now. I got up immediately and looked him in the eyes for a moment. He seemed mad at me, but he tried to pull himself together. I prepared his water for washing. In the meantime, I had eaten my food.

Unfortunately it had already gotten cold, but I had no time to warm it up again. My father had already called my name. I cleared the tub and put the rest of the stuff away and started preparing the food I had kept warm. I put the plates on a tray. You were never allowed to bring anything without apologizing first and to bow when somebody wanted to say or give you something. And you always had to put the food on a tray and the glass on a small tea plate as a coaster.

I brought my father's tray first and bowed while I apologized and said that the food was ready. I was nervous and curious to see how my first homemade food was to be appreciated.

My father ordered me to put it on his nightstand. I did, and then I got my stepmother's tray and got her a new one. I repeated the procedure as with the father. She took hers. I went out to do the dishes. Because it was also a rule that you washed up when you'd cooked I wasn't allowed to postpone it until the next day. I felt that I was very tired, but had no other chance and I'd be in a lot of trouble if I didn't. When I was alone in the kitchen doing the dishes, I had a lot on my mind. Suddenly I wondered, was the conversation between my father and Nozintombi around Grandma? Was she back in the village? I was hoping that my father might be angry because Grandma wanted us back. So many questions went through my mind that I didn't even hear that my stepmother had called my name more than once. When I heard her, I trembled and went to her bedroom.

I stood at the door and was prepared for the worst. Instead my father and my stepmother smiled and praised my excellent cooking. They hadn't even left anything today. Not even bones for our dogs, my father joked. I was so relieved and proud and happy at the same time.

My stepmother gave me her glass which was half filled with Coca-Cola and said, "Take this and sit down, my child." I took it and sat down on the carpet. Both of them seemed more relaxed to me than before. I just enjoyed it being beautiful. I saw my father the way I had seen him from the village and was so happy. When I had finished drinking, I thanked them and excused myself to go so that I could finish washing the plates.

My stepmother called Akhona and instructed her to finish washing the dishes. I got nervous again, wondering what I'd done. Before I found an answer to that question, my stepmother addressed me. She was as nice as the first night we had arrived here. She said, "My Thuli ..."' That's what my father used to call me when I was a kid. I loved it when he was in a good mood. Then I was calmer again and she said: "... you must listen carefully to what I have to say to you. Your aunt came here and wanted to take you and your sister Zoleka by force. She doesn't want what's best for you the way we want it. She told us she was keeping Xoli with her and he didn't want to live with us."

My stepmother added, "You know, you and Zoleka, you're girls and you need a mother who's there for you and loves you." She also told me that my mother agreed, and only my aunt would object. She went on to talk about my birth mother being a prostitute who had left my father because of it. It had all been all lies that my mother, my aunt, and my grandmother told about my father.

She told me she couldn't force my sister, because she'd be old enough, but my aunt wanted to bring the Child Protective Services. My father didn't say a word. He sat next to her and just looked at me. Finally, she told me I wasn't going to school on Monday because they were taking me into town to an office.

She told me exactly what to say there. I was supposed to confirm that I wanted to live with my father. That my father was loving and that I liked being with him. She also implied that my mother didn't care how I lived. So it would be better for me to live here with them. After this long conversation, she told me that I had cooked dinner very well. My father confirmed that, too. At that moment it was as if the sun rose for me. My father said afterwards that I should go to sleep now. Most of the others were already asleep, including Akhona. I cleaned myself and then lay down as well.

I lay awake for a while, and I went through a lot in my mind. I wasn't thrilled to live here forever. My aunt's health was bad too, very bad, indeed. I thought and thought," This is better for me. She's right and especially today my father and my stepmother were very kind to me." They were right about everything. Only they didn't tell me how my grandmother was. I had no choice; my father and my stepmother had made up their minds. The next day was Sunday and everyone was home. My father liked to get up early and wake us. He said with a smile on his face that girls should never sleep for such a long time. Women should be up by the time the sun rises. We laughed and got up. Today Akhona and I didn't have to help clean the house.

That's what my older sisters Zoleka and Anathi would do … Akhona and I were assigned to wear our uniforms and wash our father's clothes that he had worn during the week. It was so with our stepmother's clothes. The sons had to help my father repair his car, and the youngest son, Lwasi, was given the job of preparing food for the dogs and getting rid of what they had left in the yard. When he and my sisters were done my stepmother told him to get white and brown bread, bratwurst, butter, eggs, onions and tomatoes. He went and came back with the groceries.

My sister Zoleka prepared breakfast. I smelled the fine scents from the kitchen when we were outside washing clothes. I noticed how my stomach was rumbling and I was looking forward to breakfast. My sister called us when she was done. We had brown bread today, one fried egg each and a glass of drink-pop syrup. It tasted especially good because couldn't have it every day. After the meal, Akhona and I had to wash the dishes and afterwards finish the laundry.

Today it was also my turn to find the matching shirt and to choose suitable trousers for my father, to iron and get ready for the next day. I also made the socks, the underpants and the vest. I took the opportunity and ironed also my uniform and my shirt for school on Tuesday. When I was finished with everything, my stepmother said that I was to wash. We'd go to a mall to buy me new clothes for the next day. We took a public cab to the mall in Mdantsane. At Mdantsane there had always been an opportunity to buy clothes on the street, because there were a lot of people from Somalia, Ethiopia, Nigeria and Ghana living here and were able to live by selling their belongings. They bought me a colored top at the mall, though, as well as phalaza pants, that's what we used to call a skirt. My stepmother told me I got the stuff so I could look pretty tomorrow. I was very happy, embraced my stepmother and gave her a kiss on the mouth.

Happily we drove home again. I showed my new things to Akhona and my siblings. Then I thanked my father. We were even allowed to play outside in the yard. Akhona and I always knew well how to deal with each other because we didn't have a toy or an opportunity to play with the neighborhood kids, which was forbidden here. We were out playing our games and my sister Zoleka was in the nursery looking out of the window. She smiled at us as she read her schoolbook.

She loved to read. She also read the Bible every night, before going to bed. I liked her ritual very much because it calmed me down and helped to find myself. That was the special power of my sister, making the people around her feel safe and secure.

Under the circumstances prevailing here, it was not always possible for her to do that. Monday morning started as usual. Everyone washed themselves and got ready to go to school. There was no breakfast. Everyone got money for lunch at school. Everyone left the house and my father drove my two siblings to school.

My stepmother was also up this morning. That had never happened ever since I had been here. She was always in bed. She even ate in bed. She gave me instructions to make the beds, wipe and air the room. I took care of everything, and then I had to go back and make her bed. Then my father came to pick us up for our appointment. My stepmother went through everything with me again on how I should say and answer.

I was afraid of saying something wrong, because, after all, it was I who had to go back home with them. We finally drove off and were already expected. The woman who was sitting at the reception asked us to take a seat and wait. At the same moment, my aunt and her husband arrived. I looked at her for a moment and looked down when my aunt called my name and wanted to greet me. I watched my father and his gaze caused me to be afraid. The receptionist noticed that and asked my aunt to come into a separate room. Then a woman my mother's age came along. She said hello and asked us to follow her to her little office. I sat between my father and my stepmother. She asked briefly for our address, how we lived at home and how many kids were there. My stepmother answered the questions. The woman from the Services asked about my mother. My stepmother told her that she was living abroad with a new man. My father said he was our father and wanted our custody. She asked about Xoli and why he didn't want to live with him.

My stepmother said there were strict and clear rules. The rules, however, were by no means based on violence, but were made with love but severity. She then asked my father and my stepmother to wait outside for a moment. I shouldn't be afraid, she just wanted to calmly inquire about my school. That calmed me down. I smiled and beamed because I liked going to school and was a good student. The woman let me tell her how I liked school and what class I was in at the time. What I liked most at school and what I didn't. Then all of a sudden she asked me questions about the situation at home. I got a funny feeling in my stomach because I was afraid I would say something wrong. I already thought she was done with her questions. She asked me where I'd like to live, at my fathers or my aunt's. I answered honestly, "At my grandmother's." She asked where my grandmother was. I told her she was in the hospital, and that I hadn't seen her or heard from her since. She told me I wouldn't live with my grandmother anymore because she was seriously ill right now and she was still in the hospital. I burst into tears. She comforted me briefly, wiped off my tears and gave me a glass of water. Then we kept talking. She wanted to know why I didn't want to live with my aunt. Of course, I didn't want to say the real reason. I said just that my aunt would be very strict and I was afraid of her. She also asked why I didn't want to stay with my father. I kept silent and thought for a moment what to say so that I wouldn't get in trouble at home later. I answered that because I'd miss my grandmother. She wanted to know if I was happy with my father.

I said I was. My father loved me and my stepmother did, too. I had answered as my stepmother had guided me to. After about 30 minutes we were ready. She brought the two back in and said goodbye. We ran back to the car. When we left, my stepmother couldn't wait to ask me what the woman had discussed with me. She wanted to know every word. I didn't miss a word either.

My father stopped by a shop and went inside with me. He asked me what I wanted to eat. I was very happy, because I was already very hungry. I went for Amagwinya (a pastry), Escort and a Granadille Fanta.

I was allowed to eat in the car on the way back. My father told me I could work with him today and count the money for the passengers in the cab. My stepmother wasn't excited about the idea and hoped deep down that my father would not give in, for her opinion usually counted more than his. She had a big influence on him. She went into the house and we drove off. I felt so happy that day. My father let me sit next to him in the passenger's seat. It was like that time in the village. Then, my father had to get in line with the other waiting taxis. In the meantime, he explained to me exactly how much a person had to pay to get from Mdantsane Highway all the way into town. That was his route. During the day we drove the route from the highway to the city and in the evening we went to Kwelerha so that he could take my sister with him. I was particularly happy about it.

While we were waiting, a man came by. He sold various goods, including small toys such as yo-yos. The man put the yo-yo in my hand and asked, "Do you know how it works?"

I answered, "Yes, my friend in the village has one and I was always allowed to play with it on the way to school."

My father said, "Show me," and smiled. I did and I enjoyed it.

My father asked me if I wanted it. "It will be your birthday soon," he added. "Soon you'll be ten." I jumped up with joy and kissed him. I was happy about my first own toy. While we waited in the taxi stand, I played with it. My father also asked me if I wanted to eat something. I finally decided on chips that my dad eventually bought me. For me, this day was like birthday and Christmas at the same time. All my fears and worries were suddenly blown away and I felt happier than in the village. I also took advantage of the waiting time to play and enjoyed not having to work. For a brief moment, I was a light-hearted child. While I was still playing, our cab filled up with customers. My father told me that it was now my job to collect money, count it, and make sure all customers paid. When getting in and out of the car, I was supposed to handle the door. Everything went great and we came quickly to the city. My dad controlled the money to see if I had counted right. Everything was right. My father praised me and told me he was proud of me because I could calculate without help. He said I could work with him on weekends, too. I was very happy about that. We did our rounds, and since business was good today my father wanted to pick up my sister sooner than usual. We drove off and stopped for a quick tank of gas and I was allowed to choose something again. I had an ice cream and something to drink for the road. I was also looking for pie (meat pastry) and Coca Cola for my sister Zoleka.

We drove off and when we arrived in Kwelerha, in the first village in Kwelerha Tuba, I saw from afar Nokhala, my village, and suddenly became quiet and sad. My father just looked at me for a second and said nothing. We drove past Xoli's school and I asked him if I would be allowed see to say a quick hello to Xoli. He didn't allow it. Xoli would have turned on us and he didn't want us to see him. I did not contradict him and was again very sad. I missed everything from here, the nature, the freedom, my friends and the school. I missed the community where everyone knew each other and helped each other out. We all played together in the village and no one was excluded. In the village, everything was different from the city. My father told me he didn't want to see me sad.

So I pulled myself together and tried to smile. He changed the subject quickly. My sister was waiting outside her school. Most kids of my village went to high school here. Some also visited the school in the neighboring village, Kwa Tuba, but many went here because it was closer. I saw many familiar faces. I could only wave to them for a moment and then we drove back to town.

My sister was so happy to see me and kissed me as if we hadn't seen each other in months. I was happy and she sat next to me in the back seat. This ride flew by because we told each other so much and laughed. We talked about how they got caught when she had had her first boyfriend and had been beaten almost to death by our aunt. She thanked me for never having betrayed her. At the time, I had been working for my sister and both cousins Aphiwe and Neli, because all three of them were friends. It was always my job to open the window so quietly so that no one else would know, when at night, after visiting her friends she would slip back in the room. We talked about a lot of things. Unfortunately the journey was much too short and we automatically became quieter the closer we got to our home. My father told me I shouldn't tell everything that happened and all the things he had bought me except my yo-yo. I should also say that I'd had bread and milk to eat, only that. So that the others wouldn't be sad, he explained to me. I understood it too and kept it to myself.

I helped my father add up and sort out the daily takings since he was going to take the money to the bank the next morning. He'd also put down our lunch money for the next day already.

He gave me two rand as a reward for my good work today. He told me that the next morning I could still have my one rand so I could get a rim for lunch. I was very happy. I then went up to our room and remembered that I had a new toy. I also let Akhona and Lwazi play with it, then we went to bed. I fell asleep very quickly and was, the next morning, fresh and fit again. Like every morning, we said goodbye to our stepmother and picked up our lunch money. My stepmother gave it to everyone but me. She asked instead what I had in my hand. I told her it was a yo-yo to play with. I got it from Dad yesterday. She said, "Put it on my desk, and after school you can pick it up, and you're not getting lunch money today and tomorrow, either. Your father changed his mind. What you got yesterday is supposed to be enough for two days." She did not tolerate any back-talk. I went to school disappointed, but still happy about the beautiful day with my father. When I got back from school and when I had done all my chores, I asked for my yo-yo. My half-sister Anathi sat on the bed next to her mother and said I couldn't get this toy back, because my father had never bought a toy for a child before. Why then for me, she asked.

I stood there speechless and just sad. Anathi had nothing better to do at that moment than to add another one. She also sent me to the shop to buy her a sandwich. I didn't refuse because I didn't want any trouble. Two months later it was my birthday. I was ten years old now and had lived here for a few months already. My father had been given custody by the Youth Welfare Office.

I hadn't seen my grandmother since the day she went to the hospital. I never saw her again. I missed her very much. It was also taboo to talk about my family or ask questions about them.

I wasn't looking forward to my birthday. I was just crying and I wasn't allowed to show my emotions. There just wasn't anything to be happy about. My father called out to me and told me to wash up and put on the things that my stepmother had bought for the government meeting. When I was done, I went to see him. He sent me to take something to a relative who lived near my school. I took it and went off. I cried on the way. My father seemed to have forgotten my birthday. He hadn't uttered a word. I was very disappointed. This day became an ordeal, because my birthday was on Valentine's Day. Everything was adorned with red hearts and the people on the street were dressed red-white and showed their love to each other.

I hated that day. I hated it, and I hated having even been born. I hated my mother. I hated my life. I wished at that moment that there was a car that would run me over. It all came up again and I cried continously while I ran. Whenever I was sad, this story would come to me, the one with my Aunt Nozintombi. Since those bad experiences with my two cousins I was afraid in the night and anxious and unhappy, too. I was not myself anymore. I thought, "Mama, save me from this torment." Unfortunately, reality was different. I wiped my tears off, put on a smile and greeted the relative. I gave her my father's plastic bag. She was very friendly and gave me a little money. She said I was supposed to buy an ice cream on my way home. Because it was hot she gave me an extra glass of juice. It tasted good to me, so I thanked her, shook her hand and left.

She had been the first person today who had treated me well on my birthday, even though she didn't know that. I came back and the kitchen was locked. That was not customary when people were in the house. My father welcomed me, covered my eyes and led me into the living room. I panicked and asked myself what I'd done wrong. When I opened my eyes, I couldn't believe what I saw. My mother, my brother a couple of more aunts and cousins of my stepmother and everyone else who lived here were gathered in the living room.

I was speechless with joy. I didn't know who to kiss or who to thank first. So I started with my father, my stepmother and my mother. I was very happy to see my brother. I just enjoyed the moment because it was my first own birthday party in my life – with my parents in the same room – and it did me good, even though the feelings triggered in me were very mixed. As beautiful as the day may be, it would also come to an end at some point.

The next day, my stepmother called me to her room. Anathi, my half-sister, was also there and sat on the bed next to her. There was a tub of water in the room. Anathi said to me that I would strip off and go wash in front of them.

I refused to do it, and I justified it by saying that I had already washed myself. My stepmother told me to take my clothes off from head to toe. All of them! I did it out of fear and still didn't understand. When I was done and dressed again, I took the tub of water and wanted to dispose of it. Anathi said, "Leave it! I want to get my face washed in your filth, so I can get everything from our father, just like you. He's never bought a toy before and no kid before you got a party hosted by him, so why did you?" Before I could say anything, my stepmother spoke.

"What did your prostitute mother give you on the way?"

"Nothing," I replied and still didn't understand what was going on here. She got angry and said, "Do you think I'm stupid or blind?"

I just denied it and looked down. She continued speaking in a tone that scared the hell out of me. She began saying that my mother had gotten powers from my grandmother and she would have automatically passed on to her children. She told me clearly that my mother was a bitch who disappeared with white men and left my father and that my mother would have been jealous of my father's second marriage. I had to listen to a lot that day. She counted everything up. My mother was always considered a slut or a prostitute.

She further claimed that the mother of Munda and Bangile tried to use witchcraft to make my father her own. Thembekil's mother also tried, she said. She told me that she knew that we were going to throw her and her children out of the house later. That's why she would fight now while she had the strength. I just looked down and listened until she was done and ordered me to leave. I did and I was glad. I wondered what that had just been. I didn't believe in witchcraft but I started to wonder if there might be something to what she said about my mother. I didn't know the true story about my parents' marriage.

Why had they broken up? I only knew what my stepmother sometimes told me. I began to understand and pity my father. I wondered why Mommy had left him and why he was not happy with my stepmother. But why was she completely happy with Markus? What was true and what wasn't? I didn't get any answers from anybody, just puzzles that I had to solve by myself. I was getting used to my stepmother's outbursts and her rapidly changing moods. When my father was there, we had a guest or when we were with her in public, she was a different person. She could be, in front of other people, such a dear wife and mama. But once we were alone with her even a wrong glance would enrage her.

The week was normal, with no further incidents. I slowly got used to the rules and the change and accepted that I was at home here. One day when my sister and I were talking at home, my father called her to his room. She was there for a very long time. After a while, my father called me in. He told me to sit down, which I did without hesitation. My sister was sitting next to me with swollen eyes. She'd been crying, I was sure of that. He told me my mother was coming on Friday and wanted us to go to Grandma's together.

Funny, I wasn't happy to see my mother, but I was more excited about my grandmother right now. I asked where Grandmother was now and why Sisi cried. That's what they call an older sister out of respect instead of pronouncing her name directly. He explained to me that she was sad because our Grandma would still be in the hospital. We then went to bed and my sister prayed before sleeping.

Friday came and slowly I was looking forward to seeing my mother. My mother came and no one asked her into the house. She stood in front of the closed high gate. My father and my stepmother left the house. They spoke to each other for a while before they called me and my sister. My mother handed over a full bag of dresses for the other kids and a bag of fine things. She gave my stepmother and my father extra money. They took the stuff and my stepmother acted up on me more loosely than usual. She wished us a good time with her and thanked my mother. I stood there and didn't even know how to act. In the presence of my stepmother and my father, it was hard for me to call my mother "mama." I said hello and hugged her with mixed feelings. She hugged me and my sister and asked us into the car.

We left for the city. My mood got better. We went to eat fish and chips – that was my favorite dish. My sister wanted a kidney chicken pie. It was so beautiful. Then we were on the way to Grandma's hospital. I was very happy because I hadn't seen or heard from her in a long time. We arrived at the hospital and entered her room, which she shared with some other patients. But I was shocked when I saw my grandmother. She couldn't talk, but stared at us. I asked my mother in shock what was wrong with her. My mother told me that my grandmother was in a coma and had been awake for a few days. But she was doing well now. That reassured me a little.

She was skinnier than I'd ever seen her before. We stayed with her all afternoon and then we drove to a house Mommy had rented. There awaited us already other family members of Mommy and had already cooked. We ate and listened to loud music. Some were dancing while others had already gone to bed. My sisters and I went to bed with Mommy. We were tired and fell asleep quickly. I was very queasy, but I let myself not notice. We arrived and my aunt greeted us warmly. She had cooked dishes I'd never eaten before. I was happy to see my old school friends again, too, to play with and chat with them.

I left right after dinner. Nonkosi was also pleased much like me about seeing each other again. Later Andiswa and other children from the village came. We all knew each other in the village and played together. I brought them candy and other food. In the evening we drove back to town, because my mother wanted to be close to my grandmother in order to visit her.

We visited her every day and she made progress. She could speak slowly and swallow mushy things. Three weeks later Grandmother came out of the hospital. She needed help and care with almost everything. The first week my grandmother accepted staying in the city but wanted to go back to the village when she felt better. My mother respected her will because her health wasn't stable yet. I was looking forward to going to the village the next day. We spent a month with our mother. She excused us during this time from school. When the day came when my mother would take us back to my father, it was torture for me. I was silent the whole drive.

When we arrived, my mother asked for my stepmother at the gate. She asked her into the house. Mama gave my stepmother the clothes she had bought me and my sister in a suitcase. She took the suitcase and brought it to her room. My mother asked for my sister's ID and mine because she wanted to open a new account for me so that she could support me financially as well while I lived here. My sister already had an account and a card, which only my father and my stepmother could use. My brother also had an account but which was handled by Aunt Nozintombi. My stepmother said she wanted to go with my dad since they would have full authority over us. We drove into town on the same day and opened up an account.

My card was given to my father and my stepmother. It all seemed to be settled for my mother, and she had a good impression of our life situation. Because if she was here, harmony and love always prevailed, but this was an illusion. Everyday life was different here. Father and Stepmother were especially sweet and friendly when Mommy was around.

I had to play along, too, because I lived here with them. She also said she'd see to it that my grandmother, because of her health, could no longer look at us as before. I was listening from the kitchen while the grown-ups were speaking in the living room. My mother flew back to Switzerland the next day. Beforehand, she arranged for Qhini again to support Grandmother.

My mother sent money to get us a phone. She was willing to pay the running costs for it so she could stay in touch with us. Two phones had been installed, one in the bedroom of my father and my stepmother, and one upstairs in the kitchen next to our nursery. We were only allowed to pick up the phone if there were no grown-ups in the house.

That was hardly ever the case, because my stepmother was the one who always picked up the phone herself. Afterwards, all she screamed out of her room was, "Pick up the top!" My mother called me every day to find out how we were doing.

Sometimes my stepmother wouldn't give us the phone. She spoke for us. I hated talking to my mom on the phone, because I couldn't say anything I wanted to say. I knew my stepmother heard everything on the other phone. But my mother didn't know that I didn't want to talk to her on the phone. One day, I heard my mother asking what was the matter with me, why I was always so withdrawn and would just say hello, yes or no.

My stepmother was a pro at lying. And so she played something at my mother. She said, "Thuli doesn't feel like speaking on the phone. She is not used to making frequent phone calls" – which of course was not at all true. She told my mother that I was in a dance group at the school and that I had been admitted with a traditional dance at a dance contest.

But the case was just the opposite: she had forbidden me to do that and I was devastated, as was my teacher. Because my teacher had gone to a lot of trouble, she wrote a letter to my father and my stepmother. It didn't help. Instead, this letter brought me only more trouble, because they accused me afterwards that I would take their privacy into school by everyone knowing me after the competition. I had been so glad that I could dance and that I had been chosen. All schools in Township NU14 were involved in this competition. She told my mother that she'd like to show her how I danced, but, unfortunately, she didn't have a video camera.

My mother said it was too short notice to buy one because she'd be on vacation in South Africa next week and she didn't have a lot of money. But, with the next pay, she wanted to see that and send them one. The competition, therefore, took place without me. My mother sent a video camera a short time later. Although I was not allowed to participate in competitions, my stepmother allowed me to dance, but only in our garden. I persuaded my big sister, my stepsister Anathi and Akhona to practice a Sarafina choreography and audition.

They were thrilled and we practiced every day after school, after we'd done our household chores. My stepmother would film us now and then when we were practicing and sent the videos to my mother. My mother was happy to see us so happy and content. But dancing was all that she saw of us. She didn't know what else was going on. The days went by and I started to like it here. I only looked forward to dancing every day, because I could be myself there. One day Anathi came home from school. She brought great information. There was a big dance and singing contest in the Orient Theater and she really wanted to participate. I was so excited about it. Because if Anathi was in the contest, my stepmother would have no objections. But my joy didn't last long because Anathi didn't want to perform with our group. She picked up two other girls and practiced with them exactly what we had practiced together. I was really disappointed. The day of the competition had arrived and Anathi was not able to win with her group. It may be mean of me, but I didn't feel sorry for them. A week later, there was nothing more about dancing, because Anathi, who was in command of us, had started singing. And so we all had to sing. I didn't like singing as much as dancing, but I was not allowed to say that.

My stepmother filmed us again and sent the videos to my mother. But the singing didn't last long, either. Anathi knew two pianists with whom she finally only performed. In the end everything was the same as before: working after school and nothing else. Time passed and I was eleven years old by now. My father's house was enlarged for his sons. My two brothers and sisters, Akhona and I, stayed in the house in the same room. All the sons slept in a separate house. It pleased me, because thereby there was more space and peace in the evening, because whoever wanted to study something for school, could be in the kitchen undisturbed.

One night, when we were all already in bed, the phone rang. My father answered it. It was a doctor from the old age and nursing home in the city where my grandmother had been for several months now. She had realised with time she could no longer take care of herself because of her health. She was sad sometimes only because she'd had to leave her animals back in the village. My father had never gone with us to visit my grandmother since Mommy was back in Switzerland, although it was different with my mother. He should take us to her occasionally. It took some time, then my father called out for my sister. At first I thought maybe Mommy called.

She usually never called in the evening, especially this late. My sister Zoleka hurried downstairs. We stayed in the room with questioning glances. My stepmother called me downstairs, too. My sister had tears in his eyes. My father looked very serious and so did my stepmother. She told me to sit down. I did as I was told. She told me that my grandmother wanted to see us, me, my sister and my brother. My other cousins and aunts would already be on their way. I was happy, but I also wondered why it was so late and why everyone was so serious. My stepmother decided, however, that only my sister was allowed to go with my father. I should stay at home.

Although I was about to burst into tears, I accepted my destiny. I asked if I could go to sleep. Then, I walked out and tears started running down my face. I met Akhona and my half-sister Anathi, who brought me and they immediately asked what was going on. I said nothing, lay down, tucked myself in. My tears ran free. The questions in my head didn't let me fall asleep.

Why wasn't I allowed to go to my grandmother's, even though she wanted to see us? Why had my sister been crying before I had been called into the room? Was everything all right with my grandmother? Why had she asked for us today of all days? I almost went mad and couldn't wait for my father and sister to come back. Little by little everyone went to sleep. I was glad when the lights in our bedroom were out, and I could pull my head out from under the blanket. I listened to the night. Finally, I heard my father's car parking. I got up and opened the door for them. My sister looked down and I tried to look her in the eye and showered them with questions. She just looked at me for a second and said she was very tired. She'd tell me everything tomorrow. I saw that she had cried. My father intervened immediately and told me to call my sister and let him go to bed. He promised me he'd take me this weekend to go to Grandmother. Full of joy, as I would see my grandmother soon again, I said, "Thank you" and went back to the room. The next morning, as usual, we got ready for school. My sister was still in bed. I woke her, because I thought she had overslept. She told me she had a bad headache and she'd stay at home today. I then went to school and hurried home, because I was very curious to hear what my sister had to say. I didn't wait for Akhona today, either, because I wanted to take advantage of the time and talk undisturbed with my sister about Grandmother.

Anathi was also still in school. Only my sister and my stepmother were home. When my sister was home she undertook many of our household chores. She had a guilty conscience for letting smaller kids do so much work and that's why she only gave us smaller tasks, while she was all alone cleaning the house spick and span.

When I got home, I had to go to my stepmother's room as usual. This was a firm rule. Like every day, she was still in bed. So after I'd left things in the nursery – my sister was not there – I went back downstairs to my stepmother. On the way there, I heard my sister and my stepmother talking to each other. My sister cried and said she didn't believe that Grandma had passed away. I stopped as if frozen and did not move. Also, I cried a little. I think I stayed there for several minutes as if rooted to the ground. Anyway, it seemed like forever. At that moment, I wished for only one thing, that I had heard wrong. I continued to hear them speak, but I did not dare to enter the room. I was afraid of being punished for having been eavesdropping. I decided to go back upstairs to get a glass of water to drink and go downstairs again to have a good day.

As I entered the room I greeted them and said I would do my job now. Stepmother told me to sit down. Then she said that my grandmother had passed away. I replied that that couldn't be true, because my father had told me yesterday he was going to drive me to her at the weekend. Stepmother only said that she'd died today. Then she let me go about my chores.

I decided I wouldn't believe it until my father told me that. So I went upstairs and dutifully took care of all my duties. When my father came home that night, he said nothing, just hello, and went into his bedroom. He ate, asked for his foot massage and fell asleep. I ran into our room. My tears rolled uncontrollably again all around my cheeks.

My sister tried to comfort me. I cried all night. In the morning I was dead tired and still had to go to school. It was there that I forced myself to smile again. It was been a long day, but luckily it was a Friday. I went home with Akhona and told her what had happened. Akhona took it lightly and changed the subject quickly. I realized I couldn't talk to her about this. Although I was disappointed, I didn't let it show and played with her as usual. When we got home and greeted Stepmother, she was, strangely enough, in a very good mood.

She said to me, "You know what, we're gonna call your mama now." I was very pleased, but then she instructed me on what I was supposed to say and not say. She got me to tell Mommy that I wanted to sing at Grandma's funeral and that the camera that she sent wasn't as good as the one that Mommy had. It would not be suitable for a recording like the video camera my mother owned. I should tell my mother how important it would be for me to record my performance with the better camera.

I felt very bad about it because I was wondering how my mother would feel about this message. When I rang her, she picked up shortly afterwards and said that she'd call me right back, because it was cheaper for her. And so she did. Mommy was glad I called her, because I officially didn't like to talk to her on the phone. After a short small talk my stepmother gave me signs that I should get down to business. So I got going and my stepmother was smiling all the time and nodded benevolently to me. My mother told me that she would land in South Africa in two days and take us to her place during that time. My stepmother just said that we could use the camera to practice and that my sister and I wouldn't get back until the day of the funeral. My mother agreed she'd be here in two days and would bring clothes for all of us. The next two days went by as usual and no one talked about my grandmother. All I heard was Anathi singing and we should be standing in the background.

I wondered why she wouldn't let me go with Mommy, to be with my family. I was infinitely sad. Mommy came and brought the promised clothes and the video camera. She gave everything to my stepmother with a bright smile. I was never allowed to wear the dresses. Most of the time my stepsister Anathi wore them. Only then would I be trimmed up and only then was I allowed when my mom came to pick us up. My mother asked me in the presence of my stepmother if I didn't want to go with her after all. I looked at my stepmother and saw a "no" in her look.

So I said, "No, I don't want to." My mother was sad, but my stepmother overplayed and said: "My Thuli is Daddy's favorite, that's why she's like that." My mother seemed reassured and wanted to leave right away, because she had only just arrived and had to organise everything for the funeral. She looked very ready, but she tried to hide the pain of losing her mother. I couldn't speak when my mother said goodbye. She had tears in her eyes because my sister said she didn't want to go. For the same reasons as me. I saw my grandmother's picture in front of me when I looked at Mommy, because she resembled Grandmother to an extreme degree.

Then came the day of Grandma's funeral. It was a beautiful day. The sky was blue and the sun was shining when we came to the village. My heart was beating like crazy when we drove into it. I had mixed feelings at the time. I was glad to see all my cousins, friends and neighbors. But the joy only lasted briefly, when I remembered why they and I were there. There was a good atmosphere in the car and it made me feel angry because I didn't feel like joking.

I was so sad and I would have preferred not to have sung. There were so many cars and so many people, almost the whole village was present. The entire family of my grandmother and mommy came to the funeral. Even Norman, my father's brother, was there. We had to sing a religious song at grandmother's funeral which we had practiced in advance. So my grandmother was buried in peace and quiet. I could finally cry and grieve for my grandmother. She was one of the most important people in my life. I was thinking about the nice time I'd had with her. Tears ran down my face but in a way it did me good. After the funeral, the guests and family members said goodbye to my father, my stepmother and the rest of us children. My sister and I were allowed to stay. It was good for me that they were all here and that I was back at my village with my family.

We stayed with my mother in the village of my beloved grandmother. It was a beautiful time. Mommy took us to my father's after four weeks. She then flew back to Switzerland. So, we were back in our familiar everyday life. In December of the same year, we all took an exam to be qualified to the next class.

I learned constantly and everywhere, during my lunch break, in school, on the way home and also at home at every opportunity, because I was proud of my good grades. I wanted to learn something neat later, so I could get back on my feet. At home, however, I could never learn in peace because my stepmother always gave me something to do. Then came the day of the results. I was so excited. They wouldn't let me open the envelope until I got home. I ran as fast as I could. I gave my envelope to my stepmother, who opened it and said, "You have passed."

Thabo came in second with his envelope. He opened it and was radiant. My stepmother even praised him for having done very well. I was glad he had passed, too. Sipholazi also came home, followed by the remaining children. And they all handed in their envelopes. Everyone had passed except Lwazi and Lwando. I had gotten the best grades and was very proud. I couldn't wait for my father to come home and look at our grades. When he came, I told him, standing in the kitchen, that I passed and had got the best grades in my class.

He laughed, praised me, and ran into his room. I didn't see him anymore that day. So I finally got into fifth grade. Hell began all over again when, on the first day of the school year as I was coming back from school. I went straight into my bedroom, wanted to leave my backpack and then say hello to my stepmother. She came towards me in her dressing gown. Without greeting me she told me that today I was going to scrub the floor with a brush. In the end, everything should be spotless. As I was scrubbing the floor on my knees, her sons came and went straight to their mother's room.

When I finished upstairs, Akhona came ,too, and helped me in the living room. I went into my stepmother's room to make her bed and clean the room. The door was a crack open because the sons were in it. When I came in unexpectedly and saw the sons eating white bread with ham and drinking Cabana, they were all embarrassed and my stepmother threw the remote at me. I got out of the way. She called me and I panicked. I didn't understand what I'd done wrong, because I had cleaned everything just like she told me. She hit me with her slipper everywhere she saw me. Finally, she let me go and I ran out of the room. Then she called after me and asked me who said I was free to go. I stopped, looked at the ground with tears in my eyes and answered with a trembling voice: "Nobody." She shouted at me and accused me of deceitfully eavesdropping, and that she'd tell everything to my father. Then, in the evening there was no food for me as punishment.

My half-brother, Bangile, told me he had put half his bread in his school rucksack. I should not tell anyone. I was infinitely grateful to him because I was very hungry. I was beginning to know all the faces my stepmother had. When my dad was home, she pretended to be strict to us all and would treat us all equally. This act she also performed extremely successfully for my mother. I hadn't seen my stepmother cook or clean a single time in all four years that I lived with her. My sister gave everything to make my life a little easier. She often helped me with the cooking in secret. I was very grateful to her for it, because I was tired of cooking for thirteen people. After all, I was only ten years old. But, because of all the cooking, I, too, became a little bit more independent and a real professional cook. My sister finished her 10th grade with top marks. She was offered an internship at a dentist's and was soon able to begin her studies in dentistry. I was so happy for her and my mother was ready to support her financially in her studies.

However, my father and his wife refused to let my sister leave our city. My sister was torn apart. So she had to spend a year at home after grade 10. My uncle Maboy and his wife, who had been living in Cape Town for a year, told my mother one day that a kindergarten had reopened in their vicinity and was looking for young women who had completed 10th grade. But the prerequisites would be that they would like children and wanted to train as kindergarten teachers.

My mother shared this message with my sister. My sister was thrilled because it was not her goal to stay unemployed after the 10th grade or to get by on casual jobs. She wanted an education, a steady income and to live independently and later start a family. My sister went to Father and Stepmother with this idea in her head. My father just said, "You are not going to another city if I don't want you to." My sister wouldn't show that she was sad. She came into my room and trusted me with her plans and her secret that she wanted to run away tonight and that that would be her last chance, since my uncle and aunt were going back to Cape Town at 6:00 a. m. tomorrow morning. I shouldn't say anything to anyone and shouldn't be sad. She promised me as soon as she had an income and an apartment she'd come and take me and my brother to Cape Town.

I was sad, but at the same time happy and hopeful to get away from here. So I was left alone. When my father realized in the morning that he didn't get warm water to wash himself (that was the task of my sister), he called for her several times, but logically nobody replied. My father came into our bedroom at 4:30. He was angry, turned on the light and asked where my sister Zoleka was. Apart from me, no one knew. But I didn't say anything. My father got his belt and went after us. Then, Anathi said she thought Zoleka was with her boyfriend. She betrayed my sister, though she herself sometimes secretly went to her boyfriend in the night. My father became angry and screamed and wanted to know who that friend was. My half-sister then called his name. My father ordered my half-sister to get dressed and show him where this friend lived. I stayed calm because I knew he wouldn't find her there.

That's how it was at the time. My father, then, went to work. Meanwhile, I was beaten up by my stepmother, who called me a liar again. I would know everything and should say everything. She'd keep hitting me until I said something. She hit me, but I stood firm, and didn't want to get my sister back to this hell. I endured the beatings and didn't cry any more. It wasn't the blows, but her words which hurt me the most. She insulted me with everything. She then punished me by saying that after school I had to clean the whole house on my own and was neither able to eat at school or get something to eat at home. I didn't eat until the evening when my father was home. During this time I often got headaches and stomach pains. My stepmother told my dad I was just trying to attract attention. I hadn't missed a thing, even though I vomited due to a headache. One day she even pushed it so far that I even spat blood, because she hit me on the back with her fist. I was physically and mentally broken. I told my mother none of it the next time she called. I hated my mother a little more every day. Every time my stepmother hit me, I was angry and asked where my mama was. When I calmed down, I'd forgive my mother, because she couldn't know how to deal with my father and his wife.

About three months later, I received a letter from my sister. I was so happy and joyful to read it. But my stepmother tore the letter out of my hand before I could read it. I was just glad I got a sign from her even though I didn't know what the letter said.

My stepmother hit me and said that I knew where she had gone. Wordlessly, I let the blows befall me. In the evening she also showed the letter to my father. He didn't say anything, and I was glad. At least I would not get another punch. We ate our dinner as usual. We were already tired when my father called me in order for me to massage his feet. It was my turn today. It was fast until my father fell asleep. I went into the kitchen to put out the lights and lock the door. The sons had already gone to their house next door, except Thabo. Thabo was the third son of my stepmother from a former marriage. He was four years older than me. I asked him if he'd read much longer since he had a book in his hand. I told him I was tired and I would go to sleep. The last one had to lock the door from the inside and turn off the light. He said that the next day he had a tough test at school and he'd be studying for a long time. I should just go to bed. I was tired and I went straight to bed. Anathi slept alone in bed and Akhona on the floor.

I slept on the floor, too, but not next to Akhona, since there was more space in the room as the sons had moved into the other room and my sister had moved to a new house and she no longer was there. I liked sleeping by the window. I was asleep immediately. I opened my eyes sometime during the night and knew not if I was dreaming or I was awake. I felt someone behind me and realized his hand was touching all over my genitals. Soon I knew that it wasn't a dream but my nightmare was repeated. I just thought, "Please don't, not here, too!" It was Thabo who rubbed against my buttocks until he left his sperm behind. I lay still as I did then, said nothing and didn't resist, either. He did exactly the same thing as my cousin Songezo had done in the village at my aunt's. He came as he pleased and had sex with my body.

It was disgusting and I cried every night. Thabo also always pretended that nothing had happened. One night, when Anathi snuck out to be with her boyfriend, he came back into the room. Akhona was asleep. I was awake and had enough of what he 'd done to me. He came as usual and snuck under my blanket. I turned around and thought he'd quit when he realized I was awake. I wanted to tell him that I didn't want what he did. I shouldn't have. I couldn't finish my sentence. He gagged my mouth and pushed me down with all his might, pulled my underpants to the side and came on top of me. It all hurt so much, and his sperm was all over me.

He let me go again and said, "Don't you dare tell anyone anything!" I didn't look at him and I didn't say anything. He got up and walked out of our room. Anger rose up in me. I cried and let tears run wild. I ran into the room with my father and my stepmother, in the hope that he could save me from this agony that I had to endure in his house. I knocked and entered. I trembled all over and told them everything he had done to me. I had his sperm running down my legs while I was standing in front of them, crying.

My father called Thabo and asked him, "Is it true what Thulani says?"

He denied everything and called me a liar.

Then my father said, "We'll talk about it tomorrow. Go to bed."

I thought I didn't hear right. I was so devastated and angry that I cried all night and never slept a minute. The next day my father went to work as usual. My stepmother woke me with belt blows.

She insulted me, saying that I was a liar and wanted to stamp her son as a rapist. I'd be no better than that bitch, my mother. She forbade me to go to school that day. There were swollen spots all over my legs and upper body from the beatings. She said, "Put some clothes on, so none can see your body, Hulekazi." That meant "little bitch."

I then put on a pair of long trousers and a long-sleeved top. On the same day my brother came to visit us. He noticed that there was something wrong with me. He spoke briefly with my stepmother and told me that he was accidentally nearby in the neighborhood and wanted to visit us. He wouldn't have much time but he would have a bite for lunch. He asked if he could take me to the store nearby and give the groceries to me. My brother knew my stepmother well. If you have money you will automatically be treated differently by her. She treated my brother well when he came to visit, not like when he'd lived here with us. Whenever he came by our house, he bought stuff from the money he got from Mum because he was still at school. She agreed, because apart from me all the other kids were still at school.

When I ran to my brother, my stepmother called me to her room again. She warned me she'd show me who she was if I told my brother something from yesterday and today. I promised her I wouldn't say anything, and my brother and I went off. My brother soon asked me what was wrong with me. I started crying and my brother took me to his arms and tried to calm me down. After that , I told him everything that had happened last night. I felt very understood and comfortable while I fully opened up to Xoli.

My brother was shocked and promised me he wouldn't tell anyone. He encouraged me to be strong. He also promised to get me out of this hell, as soon as he'd finish school in a year. We went shopping for the stuff. Xoli gave it to me, we said goodbye and I went home. My stepmother was already waiting for me and asked what I talked to my brother about. I told her we met classmates of mine in the village and went shopping, that's all. I prepared the food for her and did the rest of the house chores I'd been asked to do. In the afternoon everyone returned from school, including Thabo.

He didn't say a word and ignored me at first. Then he began to humiliate me. He made fun of me saying how ugly and useless I was. He made a mistake before Akhona. He joked about me and said she was supposed to give me tips on how to take care of my vagina. I had a stinking vagina.

They laughed and I was deeply hurt, because Akhona laughed, too, even though she knew that what he said wasn't true. I went into the room and cried softly to myself. Shortly after Thabo came and strangled me and asked me what I was going to do because my daddy wouldn't have believed me. And no one else would believe me, either. I didn't say anything.

I tried to push his hands away from my neck and get away from him. He took his hand and pressed it firmly between my legs. He said, "See, I could fuck you again, you whore. If you ever tell anybody crap again, you'll never sleep again. No matter what you say, no one will believe you." He let me go and walked away.

I remained trembling in the room and came in and asked why I was shaking like that. I said nothing and wiped away my tears. My father came back from work. I was glad he was back, and I had hope when he'd come back I would talk to him about it and he would help me. But my father pretended nothing had happened. He ate his dinner in his bed and fell asleep.

I thought, "Okay, maybe he's very tired. We'll talk about it tomorrow. It's Saturday after all." But the next day, unfortunately, he went back to work and didn't return until 8:00 at night. "At least not before 10:00," I thought. But he also left his room that day without any comment and I couldn't see him anymore.

I finally went to sleep and hoped for Sunday, because he had the whole day off. The next morning, my father woke us up early and asked us to get dressed. We'd go to his older brother, Joe, who also lived in Mdantsane, but not in NU14. He lived in NU2. When we arrived, other brothers of my father's were also there. It looked like a family meeting. We kids had to stay outside, so we didn't hear what was discussed there.

When they were done, we drove back home. It was my turn to cook that Sunday. I took care of everything, because as time went by I had gotten used to cooking and doing the housework. Besides, I was already 12 years old. Four years had passed here so quickly and I asked myself what else was in store. It never felt like home. Here I felt more like a prisoner with military drill and slavery. Even as a sex slave, I was abused. I was doing my duty and when I finished doing the dishes, my father called me. I was so excited and happy when he called me. My father asked me if I was done doing the dishes, which I affirmed. He said, "Then put out the light in the kitchen and go to bed." He kept pretending like nothing had happened. He only gave one new order, namely that the sons should no longer be with us in the house after 10 p.m. and that the door should be locked from the inside. Akhona and I were then allowed to sleep in bed with Anathi. I was glad that Thabo couldn't pretend any more only to bother me when everyone was asleep. I still got nightmares at night. I got scared and panicked and wasn't my-self anymore.

Four weeks later, on a Saturday, a car honked its horn at our gate. My half-brother Bangile went there, came back and said, yes, someone was standing at the gate. My father asked who it was. Bangile said it was Mommy. My father said, "Let her in."

It was my mother and her new boyfriend named Thomas. I didn't understand the world anymore. She hadn't said she was coming. My mother said she wanted to surprise us. I stayed in our nursery and just listened. My stepmother sent Bangile out to buy my mother something to drink, and at the same time seemed a bit nervous. She came into my room and asked me to change into something else. And that's some of the clothes that my mother used to wear and that I was never allowed to wear. When I was finished, she took my hand and led me to the living room to my mom. Mommy hugged me and gave me a kiss on the mouth. I let her do it and stood still. She asked what was wrong with me.

My stepmother looked at me and tried to cover up the situation. She only said, "You know, sometimes you have to be strict, and today I'm a little hard on her." Then she took me in her arms. I just stopped and put on a smile and everything was good for everyone except me, once again.

My mother said she was going to take me with her today. My stepmother replied immediately that I couldn't go, because Monday would be school again. My mother said she only wanted me for the weekend and would bring me back on Sunday night. We drove into the village to my grandmother's house. My mother brought so many great things with her that I gave my friends in the village. On Saturday morning, Mommy took my Aunt Nozintombi for a short ride.

Soon after that, my girlfriend Nonkosi came along to pick me up, and we went to Andiswa and the other village children. We all played together and all of a sudden I didn't have any worries anymore. They were blown away for a short time. On Saturday night, when I was about to go to bed my mother came into the room. She told me she knew about everything that had happened to me with Thambo that night and that she had decided to take me to Switzerland.

I was shocked and said nothing about it. I was just wondering where she had heard about it. Then, it occurred to me that only my brother could have told her and I would confront him later. My brother swore to me he wouldn't tell that to my mother. It turns out it was my Uncle Joe's wife. She had secretly phoned my mother after the family meeting and tipped her off, woman to woman, and begged her to take her daughter out of this hell. She said to her that I was too young to tell her myself about the abuse and the maltreatment. For this I would be far too much under my father's and my stepmother's influence.

All this my mother told me only many years later. So Joe's wife had been my savior. My mother's boyfriend, Thomas, seemed very nice to me and we got along just fine. We quickly found a connection to each other. Although it had always been my wish to finally be liberated, I wasn't so convinced of the idea of going to Switzerland with my mother. I asked why I couldn't go to my sister in Cape Town. She said that my sister was busy with her career and she wouldn't think it was such a good idea. It would be too much for her.

I told her I wouldn't go to Switzerland with them and that I'd rather stay with my father. But my mother didn't care. She was not interested in my opinion, she said. She'd be my mother, and she'd had decided that both Xoli and I would go with her to Switzerland.

We didn't go back to my father's on Sunday, but instead to Norman, my father's brother, who lived in the next village. Norman was my favorite paternal uncle. My father and my Uncle Joe, were already waiting for us there. His wife and my stepmother were waiting in my father's car. Norman was there, too. My brother had to go to the house where other family members and cousins on my father's side were staying. My mother took me by the hand and walked with me to the car because no one got out. Then she said that we could begin, she'd be ready. Then, she announced to my father that she wanted to take me and my brother to Switzerland. My father said then right away that it was out of the question, he'd take me today. I was going back with him. I was just standing there listening back and forth. Thoughts rolled over. In the end, I thought I wouldn't go to either of them. My mother then laid the cards on the table and explained that I had been abused by Thambo, the son of my stepmother, repeatedly.

My stepmother protested and denied everything immediately. My Uncle Joe asked me directly: "Thulani, please tell us what's happened."

I was so uncomfortable telling that in front of everyone. I felt oppressed, forced and embarrassed. I started crying. It felt as if I had to undress before strangers. Although they were my family, I felt ashamed to tell about it so I just cried and didn't utter a word. My father put another one on top and asked me: "Thulani, look at me and tell me if you want to go with your mother or stay with us."

I got scared of him and said, "I want to stay with you." My mother got angry and said she was my mother and she decided where I lived. My father replied: "You do not live in South Africa and here I have custody of her because you weren't there for her. I've taken care of her all these years and I love her."

My uncle Norman freed me from this torment. He said: "We'll leave Thulani out of it and discuss this in peace without her." Before that, he said that he thought my mother's opinion was that she should take her kids with her. He said the stepmother's love couldn't replace motherly love. If they're gonna have her children, they should have these ones, too. I'm sure they stayed in the car with each other for a while continuing to speak without me. I was glad to get out of that car because I had a guilty conscience and sympathy for my father. I felt as if I had betrayed him.

I was overwhelmed with the whole situation. I pretended nothing had happened when I went into the house with the others. My mother then came and greeted my grandparents and handed over the things she had brought for them. They loved meat and my mother had bought some for them. Finally, she said that we should say goodbye. I didn't know what they had decided now. I refused to go with my mother and said I'd stick with my father. And, then, my father came along and said, "Let my child with me if she wants to stay with me."

But my mother took me to my grandmother's house anyway. I was angry with her and cried for a very long time because I felt very bad about my father. I was awake for a long time and my thoughts were going in circles. The next morning, my mother called my dad and asked for my papers so that she could get a passport for me and Xoli. My father refused her everything. My mother went to Home Affairs, immigration, and told everything there. That her daughter had been raped by her half-brother and her father denied her children's documents. The man who listened to my mother was stunned. He calmed her down and said he was going to help her so that she and her children could leave the country.

In fact, my mother then got temporary passports for my brother and sister and me. Her reasons for wanting me to join her were comprehensible to the authorities and that's why she also got the three temporary passports. Later, we received original passports with my mother's last name: Tomose and not Mlotha anymore. My mother travelled on 31.7.1997 with Xoli, Thomas and me to Switzerland. My sister didn't want to go because she had built up a life in Cape Town, was satisfied and loved it there.

My father remained calm and felt like a victor, because he had our documents and thought my mother couldn't do anything about it. But he was wrong about that. I was very sad and missed my father in spite of everything. I was also angry that I couldn't even say goodbye to him.

Journey to Switzerland

So my brother and I came to Switzerland on 1.8.1997, more precisely, to the city of Bern. I hated my mother and was mad at her, but I didn't show it to her, pretending everything was okay. It wasn't so easy there at first. I was living for the first time in my life consciously under the same roof as my mother and I didn't know how to deal with the new situation. Everything was different, the language, the culture. Everything was new and strange for me: only get up when I had slept well and without the pressure to do something. Mom looked after everything and made sure we felt comfortable. She went to great lengths to be a good mother. I was building more and more trust in her.

It was such a harmonious atmosphere at home. Mami's boyfriend Thomas also went to a lot of trouble to make sure that we felt comfortable. They did a lot of great things with us, showed us the city of Bern and we had common family outings. Thomas was very considerate of me, because he knew what I had experienced with my father. We also went to visit his family. They took us very warmly and we felt like one big family. I also went sometimes alone to Thomas's parents in Spiez and they did great things with me. It's always been exciting. I enjoyed it and felt comfortable. I started to like it in Switzerland, and I often went out to play with the neighbor kids. In the beginning I played with my brother at home, but we were used to being outside , playing. We couldn't speak German and the neighborhood kids didn't speak English or Xhosa.

My brother asked with his hands and feet if we could play along and they consented. From that day on, they came to us every day, wanted to play with us and they were enthusiastic about our mother tongue. They heard, for the first time, a language with these sounds. We communicated fully with gestures and facial expressions. I was more reserved than my brother back then and I wasn't the first to approach strangers, did not seek contact with them, either. I waited for people to come up to me. Then I was open.

Otherwise, I was playing by myself. In Moos, where we lived in a small village in the community of Koniz, many youngsters my age lived around. The girls were mostly 15 years old or older. They busied themselves with things that didn't interest me yet, like makeup and boys. That's why I preferred to play football with the boys and my brother. And if my brother didn't feel like it, I was busy with my diary which Thomas had given me as a present. Thomas gave new bicycles to my brother and me and we were overjoyed. Every Sunday we got pocket money for the first time in our lives, 20 francs each. Later my brother even got 25 francs. I was just happy. My brother and I did many bicycle tours together around our village and discovered new playgrounds and various farms.

I had, and still have, a very close relationship with my brother. For the first time we each got our own room. That was very unfamiliar and I had trouble sleeping alone in my room. Fear always haunted me. So I just left the light on all night and the door wide open. Whenever I was alone in the room, suddenly the scenes and pictures of my rapes would come to my mind and they seemed so real and triggered emotions in me. There was a lot of anger and frustration inside me and I didn't know what to do with it. My mother never talked about my rapes and never asked me how I felt about it. Just the one time she told me she heard what had happened and that's why she would take me with her. Nothing more.

I thought a lot about my repeated rapes and tried to find an answer as to why I had suffered so much. And I found one, too: The problem was me. I was wondering why these situations repeated themselves. Had I done anything to make my tormentors do what they had done? What had I done wrong to be treated so? I looked for the guilt in me and hated myself for it.

I cried in the night very often quietly and the next day I always felt as if everything was fine and laughed and acted normal. No one knew there was anything wrong with me. I tried to compensate my grief with food and put on weight in a very short time. Because, while I was eating, everything was fine. But after that, I felt bad. With the increase in weight stretch marks were forming on the thighs and I was only 14! My self-esteem was reduced by being overweight. I was ashamed to undress in front of my girlfriends and others, because all of them were thin and had perfect bodies while I looked like an elephant next to them.

I got to know other girls over the course of time. Girls that didn't go to my school. We got along great and did a lot of things together. Two years later, my sister came on a visit to us for three months. The aim of the stay was for my sister to gain an insight into life in Switzerland and she might eventually stay here. She slept in my bedroom and I was so happy to have her with me. In the meantime, we no longer lived with Thomas. He stayed in the old apartment and we got the apartment next door. I asked Thomas one day why we had moved out and he justified it with all the space we had now. We still had meals together and either Mommy stayed overnight with Thomas or Thomas stayed overnight here in our new home.

During this time, my sister and I talked a lot about the old times and how it was for us in Cape Town and in Bern respectively. My sister didn't like the Swiss culture and the local life and she wanted to go back to South Africa. After those three months, she left, too.

I tried everything I could to convince her to live here. But she wouldn't, because she was in love and had successfully completed her training in South Africa. We went back to South Africa with her and spent there our vacation together for the first time since we moved to Switzerland. My brother also followed the tradition of circumcision and we celebrated it after a month of perseverance.

My father also came to these celebrations. It was all good and it was good to see my father, too, when I had mixed feelings about him. He came with his family and, thus, also with Thabo.

I didn't understand why my father had done this to me, and I asked myself whether he still hadn't understood how much these people hurt me as a child. Then every time I got into a rage which I wasn't allowed to show. I was just playing happy for my stepmother while I greeted her. I pretended to be normal and polite but I was not very talkative. I played the good-humored stepdaughter and smiled and celebrated because I didn't want to spoil my brother's party. But inside I was boiling. I felt so much hatred and anger for my stepmother and my half-brother. I deliberately avoided Thabo until my father and his family finally said goodbye to us and left.

I saw Songezo, too, and he pretended what had happened had never occurred. He came to me, embraced me, greeted me and asked me how I was. I also acted normal to him as if nothing had ever happened between us. But inside me I felt differently. I felt a sense of disgust, anger and hatred. I felt powerless against him. I didn't know what I could do to contain that feeling. I had no choice but to go back to him over and over again because ,after all, we were a family. Every time again, it tore me apart inside.

A few weeks later, we flew back to Switzerland and I was glad to be away from those faces that were doing me no good. We already had, directly after our entry into Switzerland, in August 1998, started school and now had to work for the new school year back home in time. My brother went to a different school than I did because he was already 17 years old when we came to Switzerland. I was only 13 years old at the time. Since my brother had not yet mastered the German language, he attended the migration school for one year and searched for an apprenticeship as a roofer, which he also later started and successfully completed with Thomas's support.

I entered a class for foreigners in 1998, together with children from all over the world. I got along fine with my classmates, especially with Paula, who was from the Dominican Republic. In 1999, the second school year, I met a girl called Shayana. She came from Sri Lanka. I noticed that unlike the other kids, she never went home during the lunch break. She didn't have any

Znuni bread, fruit or anything to drink with her; instead she ate a lot of candy and loved chewing gum.

I spoke to her one day and invited her to our home for lunch. I also asked her about her family and she told me she had an older brother my brother's age. Shayana was two years younger than me and she was living alone with her mother in an asylum home in Koniz. They already spoke very good German, because they had lived in Germany with their family for a few years before they moved to Switzerland.

She opened herself up to me and trusted me with their sad family circumstances. I asked her permission to tell my mom her story and ask her if Shayana could come home to us every lunch break and have lunch with us. Shayana agreed. My mother felt for her and wanted to help her as well. So, she allowed Shayana to come to us whenever she wanted, even without me. But she wanted to talk to Shayana's mother first. We met with her guardian and afterwards with Shayana's mother. After that, it was official that my mother was also Shayana's childminder, and that she was also allowed to spend the night at our home at weekends with her mother's permission.

Shayana and I were very happy and proclaimed each other a sister from that day on. The second year went by so fast and I had to do the 9th grade in Niederscherli. I was still in contact Shayana and Paula. I didn't have much to do with the others in the old school after I changed schools.

Shayana and Paula came to my house sometimes and we stayed up late and talked about a lot of things. Both knew nothing of my past and I didn't talk to them about it, either. I didn't like it in Niederscherli. I felt alone and lonely. This school was different. Among the students there had been formed groups and I didn't fit into any of them. Personally, I didn't like to exclude anyone from a group, so I mostly stayed alone in the break and found it hard to keep up with the others. I used to go for walks on my own thinking about life when I had a break from school. I had trouble in the ninth grade over time because I lacked a lot of school material. I had been a good student in my home country, until I came to Switzerland. Here I had to start all over again. I had to learn the language at first and all the other subjects stayed on the route. My biggest weakness was mathematics. I decided, with my teacher, to get into the 9th grade. This is a class for students who have difficulties at school. Our teacher was very responsive to each student individually. I profited a lot from my teacher and was very grateful to her for her big heart and her empathetic nature. She had a lot of understanding for my problems and gave me everything with a lot of patience until I understood it and slowly started to feel my fear of mathematics fading away. With her help, I managed not to consider myself stupid anymore as I didn't meet the needs of the school stuff. I was the only dark-skinned girl in the whole school at first. Later on, the Muslim children of a Somali family came. I finished the 9th small class in 2001 with grades between 5 or 5. 5 in all subjects and was very proud of my achievements.

I decided to go to the 10th grade in the vocational specialist and Bern, BFF for short, in order to further improve my school performance. I saw Paula and Shayana only every now and then, but not every day, like before. I spent my free time with other friends. In the 10th class there were again other young people with a migration background in my class. I had school problems again but didn't dare go to my teacher to tell her that I didn't understand the subject. And so my grades became lower and lower. I had bad grades, especially in mathematics. I hated that subject. I felt stupid when I was in math class.

I found myself an apprenticeship as a care assistant. I went to the library in my breaks looking for the literature I needed. I was the first one to get an internship, where I could do my apprenticeship. I wrote applications and got a job in a retirement and nursing home in Bern. Then, I searched for a school and got a vacant apprenticeship at the JUVESO Bern. So I finished 10th grade at BFF.

I started my apprenticeship as a nursing assistant in 2001/2002. at the JUVESO and was very proud of myself. It all went well with my training; only with my psyche something was not right.

The Lost Sister

In December 1999, my brother and mother flew to South Africa during the winter holidays. Unfortunately I couldn't join them as I had only two weeks off from school. I called my sister, my brother and my mother at Christmas and got the great news that I would become an aunt. My sister was six months pregnant. I was very happy for her and congratulated her cordially. I also tried to reach everyone for New Year's Day, but the net was overloaded. I celebrated the New Year with friends in Lucerne. On January 1, 2000, I tried again to reach my mother but she didn't answer the phone. And my sister had her phone turned off. I tried it afterwards at my aunt's house. There I reached my cousin Aphiwe. I was relieved, because I was beginning to feel worried. I greeted her and wished her a happy new year. Subsequently I asked about my family and told her that I hadn't reached anyone yet.

She cried and said nothing. I tried to calm her down so she could tell me why she was crying, but she said nothing and cried on. I decided to end the phone call. Afterwards, I called my Aunt Nozintombi on her cell phone. She didn't answer and that was very weird. I hung up, fearing that something was wrong and finally rang Thomas. He had already tried to reach me several times in the morning, but I was still asleep and hadn't called back yet. He answered the phone and was relieved that I called him back.

He said I should come home. I wanted to know why, because it was New Year's Day and he had allowed me to go out with my friends and celebrate and come home first thing in the morning. I told him I'd come home later, that I was angry and I didn't understand why I had to be back so early although we'd made another arrangement. Still, I set off, and he said he'd come back for me and pick me up at the station. A friend of mine was with me, and I told him he didn't need to pick me up at the station.

When we arrived home, Thomas insisted that my girlfriend should go home. He'd prefer to be alone to talk to me. I replied that I had no secrets from her so he could talk. But Thomas was not to be talked to. My girlfriend might come back later, but now he wanted to be alone and talk to me. My girlfriend left and Thomas told me to sit down and asked if I wanted a glass of water.

He put a plane ticket on the table. I took it and looked at it. My name was on the ticket. I looked at the envelope and saw that the flight was already for the next afternoon from Zurich to East London via Johannesburg. I was so happy, I jumped up and hugged him. I told him that he really managed this surprise. "What have I done to deserve this?" I asked him, still in disbelief.

He just looked at me and gave free rein to my joy, without interrupting me. I asked him what Mommy would say about that as I had just one more week of school holidays. My mother would agree, Thomas replied and I shouldn't worry. He also said he'd talk to my teacher. I was so happy and could hardly wait to deliver this great news to my friend.

Then Thomas said he had something to talk to me about. Suddenly I saw him crying. I got scared and asked what was going on. He replied that something had happened to my family in South Africa.

I also started crying and wanted to know what was going on. Why was he crying? "Is something wrong with Mommy?"

He told me about an accident and that my sister had been shot. She died in Sylvester's night.

I got sick. I ran into the bathroom with my legs trembling and vomited into the toilet. Thomas brought me a glass of water wanted either to sit or lay me down. He helped me up and took me back to the living room. I didn't want to believe it. I screamed, I cried my eyes out in frustration but it didn't help. Thomas held me and tried by all means to get me to calm down.

At some point, I didn't have any more tears. I asked where and why it had happened. I stayed seated and I wanted to know everything, but I couldn't take it anymore. My nerves couldn't deal with it. I collapsed into myself and I don't know what happened next. I woke up the next morning and Thomas was sitting next to me. I was in the hospital. I asked Thomas what was happening and why I was here. I didn't feel sick. He told me I'd had a nervous breakdown and had passed out.

I wished so badly that it was all just a nightmare, but unfortunately it was the bitter reality. I felt a little calmer inside and noticed that I had been sedated. I wanted to go home and be alone as soon as possible. Thomas accepted my wish and spoke with the doctors, who agreed to my early release. They offered me other tranquilizers. I refused because I'm not a friend of pills. We drove back home and Thomas made me a soothing tea and prepared breakfast. I couldn't eat. I just drank the tea and urged Thomas to tell me that none of this was true.

He took me in his arms and said, "I'm so sorry."

I cried again and a thousand thoughts went through my head. The beautiful memories I had of my sister had ripped my heart in two. I wanted to turn off my thoughts but without success. I asked Thomas to leave me alone. I told him that I'd have to pack for tonight. Thomas wasn't very enthusiastic about it. In my condition he'd rather not leave me alone.

But I only replied, "I've done a lot in my life that you don't know about, and I'm going to have to go through that. Trust me and let me go. This'll help me."

He respected my wish and left me alone. My thoughts revolved only around my sister, our shared experiences and the countless questions about what exactly had happened.

I learned that later when I was in South Africa, my sister had visited my father briefly to receive the letter of invitation for the opening of our new delivery home in South Africa. My mother wanted my sister, but she refused, because she was going to stop at my dad's house a little longer and do some stuff. After all, she wanted to cook on New Year's Day and it was supposed to be a surprise dinner.

Later, she briefly called my mother and told her that Anathi spontaneously wanted to take her to Themba (the first son of my stepmother from another marriage), who was in the army stationed in Johannesburg and currently visiting Duncanvillage (a ghetto area). He'd be on vacation, too, and wanted to see my sister, because they hadn't seen each other in a long time. She then called again around 8 p. m. and said that everything was okay and that she wasn't coming until tomorrow.

My mother and my brother asked me to pick them up because she was pregnant. My mother also said that she wasn't quite comfortable with her decision, but she had to accept it. My sister wanted to talk to them and then spend the night with Anathi at Thembas' friends'.

My sister never drank alcohol. She lived a religious life and was content with it. That was the last time on that day that my mother, my brother and I heard from my sister. My mother got restless and wondered where her daughter was. She panicked.

She would have felt there was something wrong with her daughter. The next morning at 9:00 a. m., Themba, my father, my stepmother, my uncle Joe and Anathi suddenly appeared in front of my mother's house. My Uncle Joe asked my mother to sit down so that they could talk. My brother could then calm my mother down and she listened. My uncle asked Themba to tell what had happened.

Themba began to report that he and his friend had gone outside the night before to take their guns, shoot into the sky and so greet the new year. Themba and his policeman friend Daluxolo came over a couple of times. minutes after midnight back to the house and Daluxolo was still holding his gun. Themba said that my sister asked her not to come in with the guns. That could be dangerous. He should go outside if he still didn't have enough of shooting. He said that the colleague then aimed at my sister's head and told her he was a policeman and there wouldn't be a bullet in the gun. He'd know how to handle a gun.

All those who were sitting on the bed with my sister had gotten up, including my half-sister, Anathi, but not my sister Zoleka. Then the colleague had pointed the gun at my sister's head. She just shouted out and said, "Undigqhibile." (*You got me*). Then she'd bled from her side. Everyone screamed and ran out of the house. The ambulance had been called immediately, but arrived at four o'clock. My sister was still alive and breathing, but died while still in the ambulance. My mother looked at my step-mother, who had turned her back during the whole report. My mother realized something was wrong here. Behind the whole thing there was more to it than what she was told. Something was being hidden from her.

My mother said to Nozimbo with tears in her eyes: "Nozimbo, who really murdered my child?"

My stepmother didn't say anything. Then my mother turned to Themba. "Why did you come here first if you knew that Xoli and I had a car? We were only 15 minutes away from you. It was New Year's Day and all over South Africa until early in the morning people there are in cars on the way, which you would have if you didn't have one yourself. You should have called her father, who also owns a car and doesn't live far, either. Why did you come first at 9:00 if the whole thing happened just after 12:00? Admit it. You killed her!"

Themba denied everything and said that Daluxolo had accidentally pulled the trigger and not him. My mother didn't believe him and wanted to go to the police. My Uncle Joe tried to calm them and explained to her that he and my father had already been to the police. Daluxolo, Themba's friend, had pleaded guilty and been arrested.

My mother sat down. My Aunt Nozintombi, who had also arrived, began to cover my mother with cloths and blankets as they do in the Xhosa tribe for the mother or wife of a deceased. My mother calmed down a little, and my father went back home with his family. Uncle Joe, however, stayed a little more with my mother to help her out. He told her that he also had the feeling that something wrong was going on and my stepmother would try to protect her son, Themba. So the next day my mother decided to hire a lawyer to get to the bottom of this. She found one and he made an appointment with her and my father so that he could understand the situation.

My father agreed and took the appointment. He told the lawyer his version of the story, while my mother continued with her assertion that Themba was the culprit. Since my father and my mother didn't agree, the lawyer said that they should await the court date with Daluxolo and he couldn't do anything until then.

Back to Switzerland to me. In the evening Thomas brought me to the airport. It was a long flight. When I landed in East London, my brother and Munda, the fiancé of my late sister, were already waiting at the airport.

When I arrived, everything was different. I didn't have that homeland feeling. Everything was kind of gray. I immediately had to think about how my sister used to take us from the airport when we had first arrived there. I let my tears run wild.

My brother was driving the car. Munda was sitting next to him and talked about other things that weren't related to my sister. "I'm sorry I had nothing to do with you." They both pretended nothing had happened. He tried to brighten my mood so he and my brother talked about other things. They even tried to make me laugh.

I also loosened up a bit over time. But my better mood didn't last long. When we arrived in our village and I saw all those people standing around our house, I had a déjà vu from when my grandmother had died. Now I was twice as sad. I still didn't want to believe what had happened. I didn't think I'd believe it until I saw my mother.

I went into the house and saw my mother and the women around her. My mother looked bad. I stood there and looked at the faces that stared at me and at my reaction because I was the last person to know, and to me it was like it had happened again. I got no air and ran back out of the house without saying a word. My brother welcomed me and took me in his arms. He said nothing and held me tight. I cried a lot because I realized now that it was true, but I still didn't want to admit it.

I went back to the house a few hours later where everybody was and greeted my mother again. I sat down on the bed next to her. Then I asked her what exactly happened. Tears were running down uncontrollably. She cried, too, and started telling me everything. She told me what my uncle Joe had said to her. They both had this feeling that it wasn't Daluxolo who pointed the gun at my sister but Themba. That Daluxolo sacrificed himself for Themba and because of his profession as a policeman he would get away with a mild punishment.

I was shocked and could not believe what I had just heard. The real killer of my sister was my stepbrother who was now at large. The day of the funeral was January 8, 2000. It was one of the worst days of my life. I made the biggest mistake of my life wanting to see my sister again – in the coffin. I wanted to, nobody forced me to. She looked in a bad state. I shouldn't have done it because that picture haunted me for a long time and repressed all the beautiful memories of my sister. I remained absolutely motionless until my father carried me away. I couldn't cry from that moment on. I was traumatized, the doctors said later. I wrote a suicide note to my sister which was read at the funeral. At the end of the letter I mentioned I knew it wasn't an accident and knew exactly who was responsible for my sister's death-my stepbrother Themba.

The morning after the funeral, my father came with a gun in his belt and took his brother Joe, my brother, my stepmother, Anathi and Themba with him. My mother asked everyone who was in the house to go outside for a moment. Only the people who had come with my father, my brother, my mother, and I were supposed to be staying. My father began to speak and said that his wife very fermented would be very fermented because of the accusations of my mother's and me against Themba. All he looked at was my mother, not me even though he was talking about me.

My mother replied that they apologized for nothing because he had done that, and they knew it."And where is your pain for your daughter we buried yesterday? You're standing here with a gun and expect an apology from me? I want to be alone to mourn my daughter," she hurled towards my father and then she was quiet. My stepmother responded angrily to the fact I'd buried a letter in my sister's grave if she didn't want to accept it.

Zoleka confirmed that she would have been a good mother to all of us and her son would never have done something like that. My father nodded affirmatively.

I kept quiet, continued to listen to them and was obedient like back when I had had no choice but to be a slave at home. But then the rage began to rise slowly while my dad came up with the demand that I should apologize to my stepmother and Themba for what I had written in the suicide note.

I jumped up and forgot myself for a moment when I said to my stepmother, "You claim you were a good mother for all of us and you loved my sister? Why didn't my sister become a dentist like she wanted? Why is she pleased before you? Why is it that my brother Xoli already twice had to flee his great home and slept in water canals? Why did Thembekile, Munda and Bangile leave when they were finally strong enough to fight back? And why did they prefer to live in the ghetto instead of living in their great home with their great parents? Why can't you just be normal parents who take my needs seriously and will talk with me? No, you left me alone with my fear and my worries! And you call yourselves great parents? Why could none of us come to you with our worries if you were great parents? Right, you were great parents for Nozimbos' kids. Why haven't I ever seen you in the kitchen? My sister hasn't even once in her life prepared tea for you to drink and you call yourself a good mother?"

I did not stop and said to my father: "Since the moment you walked in here with your gun and your military gang, you are dead as a father to me." I told them they were very brave to show up here a day after my sister's funeral. I described how my stepmother had treated me as a child. How they had embarrassed me in front of her son and branded me a liar and how my blind father had supported her. I accused her of being just as much a murderer as her son was because she covered up for the murderer. I didn't let anybody speak because I was boiling with rage. I told them how much I hated them for what they had done to us. They had destroyed so many souls and only my sister and her unborn baby, no, they'd destroyed some of the rest of us, too.

I went on to my half-sister Anathi and asked her what her part in the story was. She told how she memorized the same thing as her brother. I told her only one thing: "I am not God, nor am I any judge. But I believe in God in my heart and I do promise you if you don't tell the truth and free yourself, you will never find peace and quiet in your life." I also told her how much my sister loved her and totally trusted her. I also told Anathi that she was no longer my sister because she'd covered up the murder although she knew the truth. I froze with rage and finally faced Themba. I started at him, too.

He seemed very nervous and repeated the story in different versions. I told him, "Save the lie, because I know Duncanvillage has a little hospital. It was also New Year's Day and everywhere cars were driving and people were celebrating. She tells me that she was still alive at midnight, that she died just after 4:00. You should've called my mother or my brother to take her to the hospital if it had been an accident. Why are the other two girls who sat next to my sister, nowhere to be found and no one knows them even though they were partying with you? The witnesses are you two, you and Anathi and Daluxolo." I told him he was dead to me, too.

My mother tried to de-escalate the situation but she couldn't calm me down. She got up and gave the four money to bring food and drink. I ran out of the house and felt out of place. I understood the world no longer. I couldn't understand how my mother and my brother could sit and peacefully talk with these people. I was furious! Later on they left and I didn't look at them. These people were dead to me. A few weeks later was the first court date. My brother and I weren't supposed to be there. I didn't like that but there was nothing I could do about it back then. My mother and my father took part with their lawyer.

My father was neutral while my mother continued to accuse Themba. The trial was difficult and therefore the matter was finally adjourned. However, my mother could not afford to stay in South Africa with us anymore. The funeral expenses had been high and my dad had not chipped in . My mother also had to pay the cost of the lawyer on her own. They came to an agreement with my father. The lawyer and my father would let my mother know when the court date was because she wanted to be there when the real culprit was convicted. She'd come all the way to South Africa once more.

A month later we were in Switzerland again and in our everyday lives. No one talked about the trial until the time we got mail. The letter was addressed to my mother. It was from the lawyer in South Africa. We were all very excited when we opened the envelope. Unfortunately, there wasn't a court date there but a copy of the decision. Daluxolo (and not Themba) was convicted of committing the murder of my sister and her unborn baby and sentenced to house arrest for three years. Daluxolo was allowed to leave the house only to go to work and to church on Sundays. He also had permission to go shopping once a month.

a. Daluxolo was sentenced to a community service of 12 months. The non-profit work consists of 16 hours work per month and is not compensated. Daluxolo is on duty at the Frere Hospital.
b. Daluxolo is not authorized to consume alcohol during criminal proceedings.
c. Daluxolo writes a weekly report to the supervisor.
d. Daluxolo must participate in various programs and courses which are offered by the penal system.

Where was justice? The real killer of my sister was free and the cop friend of his only received a lenient punishment, as we had foreseen. My mother didn't understand anything and she was very upset about what she just got from my brother Xoli reading to her. She tried to call the lawyer in South Africa she had hired for the on the case. But this lawyer said that he wasn't responsible for the case anymore. There was another lawyer in his place now.

So she called the new lawyer. The new lawyer said to my mother on the phone that he would not give any information, being the lawyer for my father and the mother of the deceased. My mother tried everything she could to explain to him that it couldn't be because she was the mother of Zoleka living in Switzerland. She didn't live in South Africa and had never met or talked to him before. The lawyer stuck to his testimony and said that my father had received all the information and would not provide any information. His work would be finished and so would the conversation.

I myself understood the whole thing only partially, as I didn't know English so well at the time. But I realized how upset and angry my mother and brother were. That was the last time the three of us sat together and talked about my sister. We never talked about this topic again, and everyone dealt with the loss in their own way.

My brother Xoli then decided to take my father to Switzerland for three months. I took it as it came, even if I didn't understand why my brother had invited our father, after all that he had done. I didn't understand my mother either, who had agreed with this invitation. He'd betrayed her by not sharing with my mother deliberately the information on the date of the trial, and, in addition, forging my mother's identity. In my eyes this man deserved only her contempt for all this that he had done to her and to her children. They both knew that since the day after the funeral. My sister didn't say a word to my father, let alone see him.

I couldn't stand his presence, it triggered anger and mixed feelings in me, which I couldn't use if I wanted to function normally. My father came. I didn't go to the airport because I had my first training as a nursing assistant in an old people's care home in the city of Bern. After work, I was very excited, because I knew now I couldn't avoid him and I had to live under the same roof for three months, whether I wanted to or not. No one asked my opinion. I didn't know how to behave towards him and decided to be neutral.

I took a colleague with me as a psychic assistant. She knew nothing, of course. I came home, greeted my mom and my dad and gave them each a kiss on the mouth. My father stood up and stretched out his arms to hug me. I let it happen. Despite everything, he was still my father.

We ate dinner and he told us about South Africa and about other things but not my sister. After dinner, my colleague wanted to smoke a cigarette and we went to the balcony. My mother knew I had started smoking when I was 17. But out of respect to my father I didn't smoke until he went to bed. But he had watched me unnoticed from the window and wanted to see exactly what we were doing on the balcony.

When I noticed him hiding behind the curtain, I was angry. I decided to smoke on the balcony. I thought, "Then look what you want to see because you don't deserve my respect."

My father couldn't handle my mother's upbringing. One morning when I wanted to go to the bathroom, I heard my father and mother talking about me in the kitchen. I stopped. They didn't notice me. I watched and listened to what the two said to each other. On the one hand, it was beautiful to see my parents together in the kitchen. I've always wished that. On the other hand, I didn't like the idea, because it didn't fit the image of my father in my head. I had such negative feelings for him when I had to stay at home unwillingly and he was there. I built a wall around me. I felt like I was always out of place when I came home and my brother and my father laughed together and told stories. I was angry at my brother and my mother. My mother was one day looking for a way to talk to my father in relation to the murder of my sister. Later she told me about it. My father just said we should leave everything to God and not rip open old wounds again.

The three months passed and my father travelled back to South Africa. My mother travelled to South Africa a year later and spoke with her siblings and friends there about the case. And they also told her to let the old stories rest.

That's why my mother didn't hold any grudge against my father. I didn't agree, but I tried to understand my mother. We still hadn't talked about my sister, which still made me angry and sad. During this time I doubted myself very much and wondered despite all the reasons why I felt so negative about my own father and why I was angry with my own mother who had done nothing to me. Why was I angry at my brother because he was in contact with our father? I asked myself. At that time, I couldn't understand why I felt the way I felt, and why I've always suffered from such outbursts. I felt lost and was without hope. Yet again, I tried to hide my true feelings from other people.

The end of my strength

The end of my strength was when I moved out when I was seventeen and a half and had taken my brother's 2.5 room apartment in Niederscherli. At that time, I had already begun my apprenticeship as a nursing assistant in the old-age and nursing home in Bern. My mother found a new job in the canton of Fribourg in Plaffing in a factory. And my brother got a job, too, in the city of Fribourg and both, therefore, decided to move to Plaffing, since my mother didn't have a car. But my life didn't get any easier after that. My brother had given me his apartment a few months before my 18th birthday, being confident that I'd take good care of it. But I did the exact opposite. I invited people I thought would be my friends. We made noise until late at night, even though I had to get up early the next day and go to work. We damaged items in the apartment such as the carpet, the window handles and the fridge door until one day I got a firing notice. Suddenly I stood there all alone with my worries and nobody was there, apart from my mother and my brother. Instead of being mad at me they helped me clean and prepare the apartment. I was surprised and speechless by my brother's reaction. He wasn't even mad at me even though I owed more than 8,000 francs, caused by my stupidity. And he was sitting on the debt, because at the time, I didn't have household insurance and the apartment was registered in his name. But luckily he was insured and the debt was taken over.

I was very grateful to him and I told him that I had learned from my mistakes. I quickly found a new nearby apartment in mid-range houses and moved in a week later. I set myself new goals, and I wanted to change my life. I was looking for new true friends. I only managed to live like this for a few months. I worked, went home and had no social life with friends. From time to time I visited my family at weekends. But I wanted more. So I went back to making contact with the people I called friends, wanting to get out of my routine and not to be alone with my thoughts at home any longer. Basically, I knew that these people weren't true friends because real friends for me are people who are there for me and stay with me no matter what happens in my life.

But I didn't find any such friends. I didn't care because I just wanted variety and distraction from my gloomy thoughts. So it all started all over again. We'd have parties, we'd go out, come back early in the morning and make a lot of noise. Others used drugs like cocaine, pills, LSD, marijuana, alcohol … God protected me from hard drugs, because wanting to try them didn't excite me. I didn't want anything to get my mind fogged. But I didn't judge anyone who took those drugs. I said my opinion and didn't force anyone to quit.

I was the only one who stuck to smoking weed, and, when we were celebrating, I only drank alcohol. Even though the day after I was a mess, I did the same the following weekend. I got another notice for my apartment and I lost my job, too. I was alone again, only one colleague stood by me. We decided to move to Biel together, to live and work in an apartment there and start anew again. I distanced myself from all the other people in my life and we rented an apartment together and got support from the city of Biel.

If my mother or my brother called me wanting to know if things were okay, I always pretended everything was in order. I wanted to get everything under control myself without the protection of my family or anyone else, even though I knew I could always go back home. But I didn't want to, and I wasn't proud of it , either, to receive welfare. That humiliated my pride and my self-esteem, but I didn't have a choice. I would end up on the street – without work and without perspective.

We were sitting in our empty apartment with no plan. We lived like people on the street. We didn't have a bed at first and slept on the floor. It reminded me of living with my father, with whom we'd also had to sleep on the ground. From the money we got from welfare to live, we bought marijuana and were stoned all day. We didn't give a damn about what was going on around us. One day I decided I didn't want to live like this anymore. I realized it couldn't go on like this. I asked my colleague about this and said that together we had to do something and no longer live without plans, aimless. She had personal problems and was sometimes very depressed. Often she would lock herself in her room and cry all day. I made the mistake of believing I could help her with her problems.

Today I ask myself: How do you want to help another person, when you yourself are lost and as such are running through life, don't understand yourself and can't think clearly? Sometimes I cried together with her and we locked us in our apartment. We felt we understood each other and we didn't realize how much we pulled each other down, but then it felt good – at least temporarily. I got tired finally, and I had enough of being locked up in the apartment, getting stoned and crying. I decided to go to my social worker, open up to her and ask for help so that my life could be restored on the right track.

I told her everything. What my everyday life looked like at the moment and how lost I felt. I also told her about my difficult childhood and the loss of my sister, even the rage that was inside of me. She was shocked, showed me a lot of understanding and offered to help me. The next appointments with her, however, I did not attend. I didn't even sign out. I had a guilty conscience, but after I'd smoked a cigarette I didn't care about anything again. I refused the help and wanted to do everything on my own again, but I couldn't. I got depressed and didn't want to live anymore. I just saw no sense. So I went next door to the small shop and bought myself a Godin's bottle of alcohol. Then I returned home.

My colleague was at an appointment that morning. I took all the pills that were in the house and locked myself in the toilet because my room didn't have a lock on the door. I sat down and dumped the pills with the alcohol quickly down. From then on, I don't remember anything. I woke up in the hospital the next day and was angry that I was still alive. A psychiatrist came and talked to me. But I didn't want to talk about my problems, and I got more and more angry.

The doctor realized that I was a danger to other people and sent me to the Waldau clinic in Bern. I arrived and felt like I was in a different world which wasn't mine at all. I'd rather have shot myself than be there. Because here the people were only sedated. I was kept there against my will. Luckily, I had a family who came straight away out of there. I was glad I didn't have to stay there another day. I went for two weeks to my family in Plaffein to get a clear head.

It was good for me to be in the country, and it felt like it was with my grandmother – peaceful and without the hustle and bustle of the city. After two weeks I went back to Biel and had an appointment with my family doctor, who recommended me to go to a day clinic because of my weight and my problems. He was worried because in a short time I was emaciated – from 72 kilos I was 46. I got along very well with my family doctor and his wife, who worked in the same practice. With him I could talk about my problems, too, if not all of them.

I agreed and said I wanted to try it. In the day clinic I had conversations with different psychologists and psychiatrists. After two days, a psychiatrist recommended that I go to a meeting with other patients and therapists. I also felt out of place here and had the impression that I didn't belong. I felt too healthy for this group. I listened to the stories of two or three of them, then I packed my things and left. The therapist followed me and wanted to know what was going on. I told her that instead of feeling better here I was worse than before.

She understood me and tried to convince me to stay, but I didn't want to. I called my family doctor afterwards and told him all about the day clinic he had recommended to me. I said that it wasn't the right one for me and that I didn't feel comfortable there. I didn't want any therapy by any psychologists. It made me feel even more disturbed and weak.

He gave me his cell phone number and told me to call if I got negative thoughts, like about suicide again. I went home and tried to keep order in my thoughts. I started smoking again and I was fine. As long as I was smoking, I was relaxed and the worries were less bad. That was enough for now.

My roommate and I used to go out with a girl, another friend we met in Biel. Then we got drunk and slept through the next day. As time went by, we started fighting over little things. The atmosphere between us was very tense, because we were too close and too much on top of each other, because neither of us had a job. She often listened to loud music in her room and we didn't speak for a few days.

In the apartment we were out of each other's way. Our apartment was very sensitive, because it was an old building and the walls were thin. You could hear exactly what the other neighbors did. So we also got complaints here from the neighbors. I approached my roommate about it and told her that I wouldn't want to have another apartment because of the risk of losing it because of the noise. We argued and didn't say a word at the end. Until one day the police stood outside the door when they heard loud music again. She had to pay a fine and a short time later followed the eviction.

We were homeless again. She was placed in an adult housing group for depressed people with the help of her social worker and from then on she had to live by fixed rules. I went back to my social worker and asked her for help again. I went temporarily to the Salvation Army in Biel and got a room there. I was feeling bad and really low. My former roommate called me one day and we met and made up. She told me how unhappy she was there, and that she also wanted a room at the Salvation Army. Then she got one, too.

My social worker motivated me to think positively and move on. She helped me get away from the Salvation Army. After about two months, I got a one-room apartment in assisted living. I was living alone in a small apartment with a kitchen and a bathroom. Two or three times a week, a social worker or pedagogue would come in in order to help me where I needed help to get back on my feet, live and get along. I didn't like that because I felt patronized and controlled. I discussed it with my social worker. She was able to clarify that I needed no support with the household. Rather, I needed help to rebuild a structure to get into my life and my everyday life.

She came once a week and asked if I needed anything. Most of the time, I didn't need anything. We talked a little at a time and she left. I sometimes used the time when she was there and asked if she could help me with an application so I could get back to work.

When we finished my application file, I went into town on the same day and stood up I was looking for an apprentice. The boss invited me to a taster week and she said that I was talented. I got the apprenticeship. I was also looking for a normal apartment without a custodian. I finally wanted to be independent again. I felt much more stable and proud of myself. I liked my new job very much. I got a modern one-room apartment and I felt happy and no longer controlled.

My social worker also told me that she didn't feel that I needed another care with the apartment, she trusted I would be okay on my own. I lived there for about six months and then quit it because I got a 2,5 room apartment right in the middle of town and five minutes walk to work. I was happy! I needed a new challenge. I started studying to take a car test. I worked diligently and passed the test in 2008. I was very proud.

I had made a deal with myself: if I wanted to take the car test, I would quit smoking weed. And so I volunteered for addiction counselling in Biel. The same day when I passed my car test, I also had my appointment for addiction counseling. It wasn't easy. I missed something in my life without smoking weed. The negative thoughts came back when I was alone in the evening. Quitting smoking weed was a fight for me but I made it anyway. This was a big step forward.

The way to a happy relationship

I continued to put on my smile and didn't show my true face, as usual, because I didn't want anybody to see my pain, my anger, my despair, fear, confusion, disappointment or any negative feelings. I was afraid when it got dark, because in the night I was all alone in my thoughts. I never showed weakness. When I felt weak I did everything I could to get rid of such a feeling.

I didn't want anyone to see my weakness, only my trained strong side. I rebuilt a wall around me for a second time. I couldn't get into a relationship, because that made me afraid. I was very afraid of being abandoned, but I had the urge to look for love. Unconsciously, I decided again and again to go for the type of man who was emotionally unattainable and I didn't mean it seriously. I would choose men who lied and cheated on me, but I wouldn't admit that. I wanted the guys I thought I could change by loving them. But, unfortunately, that didn't work. From my previous life I didn't know of love or trust, and so I 'd been looking in the wrong places. I started relationships that would lead to me being hurt and unhappy. I didn't know love or trust, and so I was looking in the wrong places. I started relationships that would lead to a dead end and was always hurt and unhappy. In the end, I always stood alone with a broken heart. This went so far that I even felt disgust at the mere thought of a man.

Until I met my first boyfriend. He was from South Africa and we had a long-distance relationship and we were on the phone every day. I had sex with him for the first time and he was very sensitive because I was able to tell him why I wasn't looking forward to it very much. Of course ,I had not told him everything, just that I'd been raped in the past. It wasn't easy for me, but in time he made it so that I slowly turned off the thoughts of my rape when I had sex with him. It always felt better and I had my thoughts under control.

Unfortunately, this relationship didn't last, either, because he had been lying and cheating on me all the years I'd been with him. He drove double-track with me and with another woman in South Africa. I found out that he was already in a relationship with her when he came in with me. I couldn't believe it but he even had a child with her.

I ended the relationship and was devastated. He had managed to win my trust and let me hang and lied to me. I couldn't understand that. We had known each other from an early age, for he had come from the same village I grew up in. Never had he given me a reason to distrust him. I was ashamed and told no one anything about it. So I pretended that everything was all right and it didn't matter that my boyfriend was now a thing of the past.

I told everyone else confidently, "Life goes on." But it wasn't true, because I felt as if somebody had torn my heart apart into little pieces. Then I swore I'd never fall in love again. But years later I met another man. He originally came from Ghana and grew up in Nigeria. He lived in Switzerland because he played for YB Bern Professional Football. I didn't know that at first. I once worked as a model for a friend, who was also a hairdresser, and he had my photos exhibited in his salon. He saw me there and asked my colleague about me. He wasn't my type by the looks of it, but he did have a sense of humor that I liked.

The relationship with him was relaxed until one day he was with me and told me in the morning that he had to go to Bern to get something done. He said we'd see each other the next day. I gave him a kiss, called my girlfriends in Biel and we went to the lake together. It was a sunny day and we made ourselves a cosy women's round. Just as I was on my way to the bathroom, I was attacked by a work colleague who used to have an interest in me but it wasn't mutual.

He stopped me and asked, "Why aren't you at the wedding in Bern?"

I asked him who was getting married there. And he answered: "Your faithful friend."

At first, I thought he was just being stupid, but he said, "Why don't you call him?"

At the same time, he showed me his invitation to the wedding. It said there that after two years of relationship he was getting married to his girlfriend. I got sick and I couldn't withhold my tears anymore. He took me in his arms. I let it happen, I thanked him for everything and then went to the toilet. There I locked myself for a certain 30 minutes and cried my head out. One of my girlfriends finally came looking for me in the bathroom. She called for me and asked if everything was okay. I affirmed and answered her that I would come soon, but she stayed and waited.

When I came out, she saw I had been crying. She just said, "You know what, I'm gonna go get our bags. We're going home. We'll discuss everything there in peace."

I told her everything, but I stopped crying. I hid behind my façade again and calmed down.

On the way home, my friend called. I didn't go to the phone, because I was way too angry, hurt and disappointed by him. He called me several times and wrote me if everything was okay. I texted him, "Yeah, everything's fine, just can't answer from where I am, I'll call you later."

I went home and thought about what to do first. When I got there, I called him back. He pretended, as always, nothing had happened. "Hello, baby. I miss you already, but tomorrow I'll be there. I'll see you, okay?"

I purred: "Yes, I miss you, too, and I'm looking forward to it."

He asked me if I needed anything at home. I thanked him and said I had everything I needed. I said goodbye on the phone. What a liar! He came by in the morning and was as usual. He also had no ring on his finger. He gave me a kiss. I made a cup of tea, sat down on the sofa and looked at him. I asked him how was the day yesterday with his friend. He said it was stressful and he had missed me so much and wanted to kiss me.

I couldn't stand this act any longer and I said, "Look in my eyes and tell me if you married another woman yesterday." He looked at me and denied everything. I asked him to give me his cell phone. I've never had that before. Either you trusted each other or you didn't. He refused. I gave him a choice. He either gave me his cellphone or he should disappear from my life forever.

He said, "Well, then, I'll tell you the truth myself. You are right about the marriage, but it didn't happen out of love. I love only you."

I was shocked, felt nothing and did nothing. When I came to I said to him, "Do you see those tears? They flow for I was stupid to trust you and to love you more than myself. I feel sorry for this woman you married. She thinks she's got a husband, but she's only got one cheater. I wish you all the best for your future." Then I added: "I don't go to church like you, I don't read or occupy myself with any Bible, I go to no prayer meeting, I don't know any Bible verses, but I do believe in God with all my heart and I know that God is not a deceiver and does not lead people to such deeds, but rather that is man himself with his ego, and he hides himself behind religion. God is just and sees and acts out of love. Everything you do to a person, you get back, I promise you." I felt really bad. I wanted to get my peace from the men and all other people. I couldn't feel my pain with my mother, who realized that something was wrong with me. I couldn't talk to anybody about it, not even my friends. My friends didn't know much about me anyway.

I hardly ate anything, my appetite had faded. I locked myself in the apartment and didn't want to see anyone. I was weak and I fought that. With my last strength I went to my brother and asked him for advice on how to forget a man. My brother gave me a piece of advice for which I've been grateful to him ever since. He said to me, "The only way you can forget him is to go on with your life as you have been doing and thus, you will never lose sight of your goals and it will never be hard on you. Never be dependent on a man in any form whatsoever."

I took this advice and slowly found my way back to my old life. I worked and finished my apprenticeship as a hairdresser. Time passed and one day my colleague convinced me to sign up for a chat dating site. She thought that I was too serious, and a little flirting wouldn't do me any harm.

In a very short time, many men wrote to me and made me compliments, but I quickly realized that many of them were more into looking and sex. Again I had to explain to them that I wasn't merely an object, but also possessed feelings myself. I wasn't online much. Sometimes I'd look at the chat once in a week and, then, there was mostly much to read. But I didn't care, because I wasn't looking for fast sex. I seemed pretty much the only one at the time: Many users of this chat site just wanted sex. Repeatedly they offered me money for sex or asked me whether I could send my underwear. That was just the tip of the iceberg. When I read it all, I wondered if true love ever existed in this world. A lot of my girlfriends didn't understand me.

I got off as stupid because I refused all those offers and I didn't want anything to do with these men. But I have my pride and my faith and I never had any of this with my conscience. They said I would do it for fun but I didn't want that. My goal was not to play a game, but to have an honest relationship.

One day, a boy from Germany wrote me a letter. He was the complete opposite of all the men I'd known so far. He talked about normal things and wanted to know a lot about me. We even started to Skype. The boy aroused my interest and we spoke daily before going to bed via Skype and it felt like it was good. I got used to talking to him every day. He contacted me several times a day and I had a good feeling, but fear still haunted me. He came to Switzerland one weekend to meet me. When I met him, I felt nothing and I wasn't nervous. I was calm and it wasn't love at first sight, but I liked his character, and I warned myself not to lay too much emphasis on looks and give him a chance to get to know me.

We got together and he got a job in Zurich and also asked me to move in with him. That scared me in the beginning, because so far I had always been self-reliant. I was open to a new love and wanted a family, too, but I was still on guard and ready for anything so that I would never be hurt again by a man again. But he tried hard.

Both of us were united by the desire for our own family. We decided to have a child. So came our son, Shane, to the world on 11. 06. 2010. A little while later the father of my child proposed marriage in South Africa on vacation. It was very nice. But when we got back from vacation I saw that things weren't right between us. I found out that we were very different. I thought we knew each other through our long-distance relationship, but that was a fallacy. In retrospect, I realized we didn't really know each other. We fought more and more often because of trifles and disagreements. We had completely different ideas about life. I wanted, for example, to pursue a career in addition to my job as mother. He, on the other hand, wanted a housewife dealing 100 % with the child and the household.

We didn't find balance in our relationship. I don't blame him or myself for the fact that our relationship failed. I thank him for the wonderful gift of my son Shane. Shane is my pride and joy and I will always respect the father of my child. Meanwhile, I'm glad we broke up, even though I had to start all over again. I had to take off as a single mom. I went back to Bern and moved into the same street as my mother. Shane's father went back to Germany.

I was given a place in a nursery in Bethlehem in Bern. Then I was to come up with a plan B, because the salary as a hairdresser wasn't enough. Besides, there was the fact that all the employers wanted someone with experience. Of course I didn't have it because I had become a mother right after my education. I contacted the Swiss Red Cross, SRK for short, looking for an internship in old people's and nursing homes near me.

In fact, I quickly found something. After six months, I finished my internship and the school at the SRK. I applied there right after taking the exam at the SRK and received a part-time position of 70%. I was happy. I had agreed with my ex that he would take our son every other weekend and bring him back. It cost me a lot of patience and understanding to get along, reconcile and be friends with him in order to make a somewhat normal company. But this was all about our son. Not for me, not for him. I didn't want my son to experience the same thing

I had when I was a kid. He should grow up normal, with mother and father, even though we had broken up.

It worked most of the time, but not all the time. He was also happy in a new relationship and I was happy for him that he'd found what he was looking for. I was busy with my kid, and that was what it was like.

My son is a gift from God to me. He gave my life meaning again. He's six years old now, has started school and I'm really proud of him and me. He calls himself big but to me he's still small. The love that he has is bigger than anything else in the world. After years, I tried various dating events and quickly realized that I wasn't in the right place. I was very concerned with my expectations and ideas of a man in my life, because I had changed a lot and I now knew what I expected from a relationship. So I quickly decided to delete my profile on all the dating pages, focus on me, and remain single.

I've discovered for myself that it doesn't do any good looking for someone on a dating site. I'm not suggesting that it can't make an exception, but I've learned that this is not my way. I like it a lot better to have a natural way to meet a man. The dates on the internet are superficial and that's not good for me. I've discovered myself and my worth so now I can deal with my single life differently and be happier. I'm working on my new life instead of desperately looking for someone.

I started with fitness and wrote a lot about my life. And so, the desire arose to write a book about my life. I set myself a goal and wanted to keep up. I spent a lot of time with myself, doing what I'd never done before. I got to know me and thought a lot about my life. I felt free in my soul and after three years as single I was ready again to open myself to love, because now I knew what I wanted, what did me good and what didn't. I was used to not looking after me and putting me all over the place. This should stop now!

I had stopped looking for a man because all these years I had been looking for myself and confirmation that I don't need now anymore. I had finally found myself again, knew my worth and now knew what I have achieved in my life. I wasted a lot of

time with people who weren't worth it and my heart was broken several times. It took me a long time to realise that I wanted
to change myself for other people only to make them like me.
I lived into the day and threw myself into work and life. I met
good and bad people on my way and don't regret that because
they all gave me valuable lessons for the rest of my life.

The accident

My brother called me on Friday, August 8, 2014, after work. I had just completed my training as a health professional. I was tired. He asked me if I could take him to Yverdon in his car the next day since he had lost his driver's license because of speeding.

I consented, though I was tired from the week, but my brother had always done everything for me. I picked up my son at my mother's after late duty. On Saturday I drove my brother to his best friend Ally, who was in prison at the time. Since I didn't want to go to prison with my son, I drove home again for 40 minutes and had a short nap. I arranged to pick my brother up after three hours.

I suddenly didn't feel like going back and my mother told me on the phone that I should listen to my feelings and tell my brother that honestly. He'd understand. "You 've already driven him there, after all. Tell him to take the train back," she added.

I said to her, "No, I'll keep my promise."

My mother asked me to wait for her. She wanted to keep me and my little prince company in the car. But I refused. Shane drank something in the car and I drove back. At some point I missed the exit and didn't know where I had ended up. My brother called me and wanted to know where I was. I said I didn't know exactly, but I'd find the way. Then I found my way around, too. I flashed to turn left and had to stop for the right turns. That's the last thing I remember.

It came all like a dream when I heard from far away my son screaming out loud to me. Then many lights danced before my eyes and people shouted my name and repeated that I should stay awake, but I couldn't. I fainted and woke in the ambulance later.

"Where's my kid?" was my first question. I panicked, I fought for me and asked, "Why am I here?" They told me I had a head injury, and they were taking me to the hospital. I passed out again and from that point on I couldn't remember anything. I awoke after two days, but reacted to nothing and I couldn't remember anything. I had my eyes open. My mother later told me that my son to see me.

My son said to my mother: "Khulu (grandmother in Xhosa), Mommy's dead." They kept my son for one night for observation at the hospital. It quickly turned out that he was unharmed. I couldn't remember anything. My family told me that after two days in Yverdon I would be relocated to Bern in the university hospital. There was an intensive care unit there.

My head injuries were severe and everywhere I went I was hooked up to tubes. I had an accident with a motorcyclist but I couldn't remember how it happened. From August 9th to 19th, I have a memory gap. I woke up in the intensive care unit in Bern. The hospital staff asked me my name, but I couldn't utter it. I just didn't know it. I was disoriented and had no memory. My head was empty and I didn't understand everything.

At first, it was incredibly hard for me to understand the meaning of a sentence. They asked me my name several times a day until I knew what my name was, but I felt no connection to that name, didn't know who I was and what happened here. I was foggy with all the medication I was on in order to endure my brain trauma and shock.

After a while they transferred me to a common ward because I was finally able to answer. But shortly afterwards I passed out again. Again I woke up dizzy in intensive care and something was burning between my legs. I reached over there, where it hurt, and found that I had been given a catheter and I'd put it on the ground. My mouth and tongue were sore and hurt. I asked a nurse where I was and what had happened. She told me everything about my car accident. But already after a few minutes I had forgotten everything again and that upset me.

The nurse was very patient with me and told me that I should calm down, everything would be fine. I had an epileptic seizure, but after a cerebral hemorrhage that could happen. I didn't quite understand what she meant and slept exhausted. After three to four days, they moved me again but I had another epileptic seizure. When I was reasonably stable, I was sent to the Anna-Seiler rehabilitation center.

The memories came back quite well even if only blurred and patchy. I wasn't allowed to get up alone and had to ring when I wanted to go to the bathroom. If I wanted to take a shower, I needed support and I had to sit on a chair because of impaired balance and double vision. It always did good to feel water on my body and not only be washed in bed by nursing staff. I was prescribed various therapies, as well as ergotherapies, neurological therapies, physiotherapy and speech therapy. I got it all written down because I still had to try hard to remember little things. I also got an agenda with photos and names of the doctors, of the nursing staff and the therapists, because I could not remember any names.

My schedule was on a timetable. I felt like a child who had to relearn everything. I was angry about this big backward step, because I had fought hard for my successes, also for my further education to health specialist. It upset me to think I couldn't even remember a name. I panicked and thought I'd lost my mind and with it my life. I was thinking if I keep forgetting everything would I ever be able to understand and retain the subject material? How could I handle my kid on my own?

All these questions I just couldn't get all these questions out of my head. When I had neurological treatment , it was especially bad, because that's where I noticed most of what was going on in my head. I forgot everything about the test again and everything that was shown to me, whether they were pictures or simple words or names of persons. I was devastated. Besides, I wasn't allowed to go anywhere unescorted. I couldn't stand the hospital any longer. I felt like a prison inmate. I even had to walk from the room to the hallway and run back several times to be able to remember this.

I practiced this with the nursing staff and the therapists. They did their job well and were very patient and indulgent with my unsettled moods. I didn't want to concern myself with the fact that I had lost my mind and so I left my frustration at the staff off. A therapist told me one day when I was desperate that I had a serious problem. I had severe head injury and head trauma, as well as brain hemorrhage on the right side of the brain, where the emotional centre lies. And that's how I understood why I had mixed feelings and had no control over my emotions anymore. I asked my neurologist to explain to me in more detail what had caused the accident in my head. She was a very empathetic woman, who did not only do her job but she looked after her patients with all her being.

She told me my memories would be coming back. I'd just have to be patient. But she also said that it could be that my outlook was difficult for the time being. I was horrified and wept my frustration from the soul. There were days when I understood that I had a problem in the head , but sometimes I also switched to draught and I didn't want to understand why I should stay. I cried a lot and was given medication for the mood swings. Before my accident, I hated to swallow pills. Now it was five to six pills three times a day.

The doctor said I would have to spend a total of three months in rehabilitation. That would be necessary to make my brain recover. I felt as if once again the floor had been pulled out from under my feet. I felt lost and became depressed. I was sluggish and had no motivation to go on. I was wondering what my future would be like and what would happen to my child if I didn't use my mind.

Time passed too slowly. I didn't read the news. I didn't watch television, either, because that was much too exhausting for me, as I saw everything double and didn't understand what I heard and saw right anyway. I was cut off from society and my life was all about the hospital. Even though I was back at a low point in my life, I neither could nor didn't want to give up. I've been able to get through the worst of times in my life and the strength to go on, and that was exactly what I wanted now. I remember the day I was with the chief doctor, the senior physician, the ward manager, my physician and my neurologist and therapist at the same table. They were trying to explain to me exactly what my problem was. They said that it would be very hard for my injured brain right now to put everything in order. They said that I had suffered several traumas in my brain and all these feelings and experiences I'd had would be refreshed through my brain injury.

I needed somebody to give me hope again and to put the strength in me again. I felt that all the patients had been treated equally. They were all asked the same questions. In therapy, most therapists used technical terms, with which I could not come to terms much at this time. During their rounds doctors came in wearing their white coats, with a sheet of paper in hand stood around me. They asked me questions like how I was after the accident. I always replied that I was fine, because it was completely unclear how I was going to be able to face all these people, interns, to summarize my true feelings in a short time and answer honestly.

I didn't show anything; everything was fine on the outside. I felt that sometimes in such situations I was losing my mind. I had the feeling they didn't really want to know how I was doing, but were only doing their duty as a rule. It was at these moments that I began my career as a nursing assistant and budding health professional. Was that really a profession for me, a profession I wanted to learn? Because I wanted to help people, I wanted to have time for my patients. I wanted to understand their worries, and not leave them alone with their questions and fears that would lead to new problems. Of course, there were staff here as well who put their hearts and souls in the job and you felt understood by them and you felt they didn't leave you alone. It was good to have someone in my room who just had a little time to listen to me. I appreciated these people. They were angels to me.

One day, when I had another consultation with my neurologist, I couldn't take it anymore and did what I should have done a long time ago. I opened up to my therapist. I told her that I was tired of being asked how I felt and that I was immediately labeled depressed if I answered honestly. I told her about my past and lamented that no one understood me. But how could they see what tortured me not being able to look inside me?

She took me seriously. The therapist listened to me, gave me a glass of water and a handkerchief to wipe the tears off. For the first time, she made me feel understood. I told her I'd seen some bad things in the past but still, after every blow of fate, I kept getting up and going. But right now I couldn't see the end of the tunnel.

She said to me, "Mrs. Tomose, you're a brave woman, even if at the moment you, having been through the experiences and the accident, are incapable of recognizing that. But in the future you will see what you've fought for so far." She told me she'd understand better now why it was like that and what was going on inside my head. She also understood my frustration and anger at the doctors and therapists. She understood that my outbursts of rage had been misjudged, for they came alone out of the helplessness that I felt. She then organized a session with the ward physician, the therapists and nursing staff to educate them about me, so they'd understand me, too. I was very grateful to her for that.

So the first weeks went by and I learned a lot about myself, other patients, the doctors and the nursing staff. Here all age groups were represented and the other patients suffered brain injuries, as did I. I became friends with Johannes, who came from Germany and had been in the same ward as myself for some time. Also, he had a brain injury. He had been hit by a car and, like me, had lost his memory and his sense of balance.

He still saw everything double. I also got along well with Michael, who was wanton and had been run over in revenge. Hans-Peter was one floor below us and we also understood each other finally. He had a tumor that needed surgery. Daniela was also on the same floor as Hans-Peter and had a stroke, and had really forgotten everything. We made fun of our injuries, confusion and partial disorientation.

There was another guy whose name I have forgotten. He had a motorcycle accident and his head was open. His skull was held together with a helmet and the missing skull pieces were kept cool until surgery. He was our comedian and made us laugh all the time. He also made a lot of jokes about his looks after the accident and the fact that his skull was in the fridge. He used to say he'd have a frontal damage.

These people did me good. We started eating lunch together instead of being lonely and alone in the room. It helped me very much to exchange experiences among one another and speak about our frustration, our fears and our lives. As different as we all were we formed a sworn troop. If we were in a bad way, we cheered each other up and took each other for a ride. The others liked to make fun of me, too, because too much information at once quickly exhausted me and I always had to take a nap. Even the common lunch was sometimes too much for me.

In this group I noticed that a professional title doesn't make people better or happier. There were all types of people with injuries. Rehab did me good. I learned a lot about myself. I learned to be more patient with me and not want to do everything alone. I learned to accept help. It wasn't easy for me because I had fought alone for myself for many years and never wanted to accept a helping hand. I saw my situation as happiness in disguise. Finally, I would have died in the accident or suffered worse injuries.

There was a pastor who came to see me, as well, to listen for an hour. She was interested and went with me often out in the fresh air. We walked together through the surrounding parks and gardens. She was trying to sweeten my everyday life a little. I liked her calm nature and I felt understood. One day – I still remember very well – I walked with her to a cemetery and there I suddenly thought of my sister. I told her about my memories and the feelings that surfaced. She listened to me attentively and gave me the impression I was understood. Even though I was in the company of these wonderful people, I was still very unstable. I was lost for so long through life, even though I had everything on the outside to lead a happy life. I had a permanent residence, I had completed two training courses, I had a great mother, the best brother you could ever wish for and a wonderful and sensitive child. I should be feeling happy, but I didn't. I functioned perfectly on the outside but on the inside everything looked different and nobody could see it.

From doctors or psychiatrists I got, time and again, the recommendation that it would be better for me to take medication such as antidepressants or mood enhancers. I didn't think much of it and I deliberately refused, because I wanted to understand how I functioned and how I could find solutions to my problems. I wanted to fight the cause, not the symptoms. After more than two months in the rehabilitation clinic, I left the hospital grounds for the first time.

We walked at the beginning, because I was afraid of everything that drove. I didn't have orientation at first and I couldn't remember the way. That made me scared. We then practiced driving to a station by tram from Loryplatz to Schlossmatte. My heart raced and I began to sweat. I was happy every time I got out of the vehicle. We kept practicing diligently until it worked out reasonably well. I made progress. Soon after, the doctor said I was supposed to go home Friday night till Sunday night. I was very happy about that. My mother, my brother and my son got me the first weekend and we went to my mother by tram. Everything was so strange to me all of a sudden.

I asked them to accompany me to my house. I wanted to see my home. As we walked along the way, a car stopped. The man at the wheel was pleased to see me and I smiled back and greeted him. He asked me how I felt now. I said, so far so good. I was glad that I was still alive. Then we said goodbye and he drove away. I told my mother I had no idea who it was. I knew his face but I couldn't remember his name or connection to him, which made me feel uneasy.

My mother tried to calm me down by saying: "Look what's come back to your mind. You'll be fine, you just have to be patient." When I opened the door at my house and went in my apartment, I suddenly felt a mixture of sadness and confusion inside me. Everything felt strange. I went into my bedroom to get some clothes for the hospital. On my bed there were still my schoolbooks, just as I had left them before the accident. I couldn't hold back my tears any longer.

My mother came in, took me in her arms and asked what was going on. I told her that I had just realized that I could have died and never come back. Then what would have happened to my child? To my family? I couldn't stand that in my apartment and wanted to go back to my mother. I felt more comfortable there than at home. On Sunday I drove back with my family. I was back in rehabilitation and received my weekly schedule of therapies. Already the next day I had another consultation hour in neurology. I told the therapist about my visit to the house and how I had fared. She was trying to explain to me that no one could tell how quickly my brain would recover from the accident. She said I shouldn't lose my hope after all I'd been through.

I felt understood and we conducted the therapy though I was still having trouble retrieving things in my brain. I just couldn't make it. That frustrated me even more. I went back to my room and my phone rang. I picked up the phone and it was my dad, with whom I hadn't had any contact in years. I was shocked and didn't understand how he could have called my phone number and why he acted as if we'd only spoken for the last time yesterday.

I was confused and hung up. I decided to call my mother. I told her what had just happened and I asked her what was going on. She told me that she had given my father my number. I was angry and yelled at her and hung up on her. She tried to call me again, but I didn't answer. Then my brother called and I told him that I felt betrayed by Mommy, because she knew that I didn't want any contact with my father. My brother replied that he'd come by and we'd talk it over in peace. I agreed.

My brother came with Mommy. I went to the lounge with them, where there was no one, because I wanted to be undisturbed with them. Mommy explained to me why she gave my father my number. She said she was afraid and thought it was not fair not to tell him that his daughter was at the hospital. I stayed calm and listened to her until she was done. I said how angry and disappointed I was. I knew the time had come now to tell my mother and my brother everything. That's how I told them about my whole childhood.

"Maybe now you'll understand why I'm not so thrilled about my aunt and her son, your nephew, who brutally raped me. Afterwards, my stepbrother also got sick of me and my father didn't help me." I left nothing out, and my mother couldn't keep her tears from her eyes and cried for a long time. My brother was angry. He couldn't listen to what had happened to his little sister. I told my brother it didn't do any good now to get back to these people, after so many years, because I knew that they would receive their just punishment.

I told my brother to calm down and not to do anything. I'd like to do something about it. The punishment they deserved would be what they would get. I don't believe in violence and revenge but I believe in God, who knows what justice is. I told him that if I didn't have my faith I might have become a killer myself. My mother just told me that she didn't know anything about any of this.

She knew how I felt about my stepmother but she did not know about the rapes and the abuse. She cried a lot and wanted to take the blame.

I said to her, "You're the one I want you to be. I'm the one you feel most sorry for because you trusted these people whom you loved and who betrayed your trust. Just to get your money, they pretended to be a loving aunt, an understanding stepmother, a good father and great cousins. You're the real victim in this story." I always got angry when she protected her sister with money. I didn't know what to do with my anger when I saw her helping Songezo with his training. Not that I didn't begrudge anyone anything, but he didn't deserve it!

I've had a lot of outbursts of rage when we were on vacation and we played happy family . These people pretended nothing ever happened and that almost got me and felt despair. Because everybody thought I was crazy or I too vindictive. It was good for me to say everything. In the end I felt liberated. Now I never had to pretend anything for my family again. For the first time I felt really freed from my inner war.

Rehabilitation was slowly improving. I had good and bad days. My emotions were sometimes crazy during this time but my progress made me happy and I counted the days until I was released. I went to my workplace with the ergotherapist in order to discuss my reinstatement, because I wanted to go on with my life straight after hospitalization and continue my education. I wanted to live independently without any financial support from the city. My pride didn't allow me to take money from the state, so I made every effort to get back to work. In the interview with my ergotherapist and employer it turned out that at first I should be working only two hours a day.

I agreed and looked forward to starting work very much. I continued my therapy, met a man and also had memory therapy with him. We got along well and I wanted to learn a lot about the human brain. He explained everything to me patiently. He was the first person, apart from my family, who I also saw outside the hospital and didn't make me feel uncomfortable.

He cooked, we watched a movie together and philosophized about life. What united us were the deep conversations about life because he, too, had not had a beautiful childhood.

One day he said, "You're the best therapist for me I've never known."

We were treating each other in a way, and that helped both of us a lot. We also felt each other physically attractive, but at the time, I wasn't looking for a relationship because I've had enough to do with myself. He told me that he'd been single for six months and he did not have a relationship right now. So, it was a great fit between the two of us. He brought me in on my last day of rehabilitation and we went into town for a drink. I felt safe in his presence, because he knew what I had, and I didn't have to be afraid. I invited him to my place a few days later and we cooked something. We sat together and talked a lot. It was a beautiful evening. And then we couldn't get our hands off each other and he just kissed me and I kissed back and it happened. I spoke to him about it the next morning. I told him that I didn't actually go to bed with a man who wasn't my partner. But now it had happened, and we were grown up enough to straighten the situation out, because to me friendship would not fit with sex.

In the end, we decided on a friendship that unfortunately didn't work. I let him go but I was very happy to have met him. I learned a lot from him. That's why I felt no grief or anger. I felt more compassion for him because he didn't realize that he needed help to accept and love himself so that he could be able to accept and love others as well. I knew how fast it could happen, that something was going on inside you and you did not notice that it was not true and that one's own feelings were manipulated from the outside. I've learned to distinguish people from each other through my past. Those who did me good, and those who did me harm.

I broke up with the latter. During this time I got to know valuable people, whom I value very highly and I'm grateful to have in my life. People who accept me as I am now. I decided to leave the hospital right after I was discharged. I don't have time to lose at the hospital. Thus I started work a month later. I went there twice but working in this department didn't fit me anymore.

It came how it had to come. We made a termination agreement by mutual agreement and it didn't feel like a loss, but like a liberation. I left voluntarily because I had learned to listen to my inner voice. When I was on my way home I decided to reapply. Arriving at home I started to look for vacant apprenticeships immediately. Soon after, I was sent to an interview to a dementia ward. I was quite frank and honest with them and told them all about my accident. I told them I wasn't very resilient yet and that I got tired quickly. They let me walk on the station for two days and they were satisfied with the way I treated my patients. I got great feedback from the head of the department and received the apprenticeship in August 2015. I was very happy but at the same time I had great respect. I was on a dementia ward again and there you have to be especially resilient. I got an introduction and started working independently afterwards but also had a learning guide. I liked working there very much, and at work and at school everything went smoothly.

I felt very comfortable. Nevertheless, I could sense that I was running at the limit. Every night I suffered from severe headaches. In addition, after the already strict workday I was expecting another child at home. I wanted to take care of it, of course. Not to mention the homework, which I also had to take care of. I didn't want to admit that at the end of my rope. I had my goal in mind, that is to make the training to become a health specialist and to work independently and without state intervention.

Two weeks after taking up the job I had an epileptic seizure at work. For a year I've had no seizure. Since my first seizures back then in the hospital I had to preventively take a pill three times a day. I woke up hours later in the hospital and knew not what happened. I was confused. A doctor came to me and asked me a lot of questions. I was quickly released again and my mother and my brother took me out of the hospital. I stayed home for a few days afterwards. My mother and brother stayed with me for the first night.

After two days I went back to work. My boss showed a lot of understanding and stopped me when she saw me tiring. She also spent time talking to me. I went on but my headaches didn't go away. Then I went to my family doctor for a follow-up and he referred me to Salem Hospital. I explained exactly my problem to the neurologist there, and that my mood had also deteriorated. I was often edgy and suffered from depressive episodes. I took medication for my mood swings by the psychiatrist I had been referred to after the accident. Then my mood got better but it caused me to drop out and I suffered from constant fatigue. I told the neurologist everything and that I didn't want to continue this therapy with my psychiatrist. The neurologist agreed, because he had the feeling that it was more than just an ordinary depression. Also, he didn't understand why the psychiatrist just thought I was depressed instead of trying to understand what was happening in my brain. Yeah, I've had some mental problems, but they were not cured and got worse from my accident.

My neurologist recommended two attending physicians who worked in the clinic of Wyss. I quickly got an appointment with a senior physician/psychiatrist and felt comfortable and understood from the first day. Her name was Dr. Leiva. She wanted to get an idea of me, so I told her about everything. After a long investigation and our conversation she recommended that I reduce my workload a bit to avoid the stress in my head which could trigger these epileptic seizures. She told me to stay here for four weeks to be treated, because she recognized my problem from the beginning.

There was also a termination agreement this time but I knew that sooner or later, due to my instability I would've gotten to it anyway. I was sad at first, but with the help of Dr Leiva, I'd never given myself the time I needed in my life. I had always only functioned – and that was good, but inside me I was a wreck. From January 2016 I was officially unemployed and 100% on sick leave. I went to see Dr. Leiva once a week and we started all over again in my life. It did me good to take time on that and I realized how much all this was making me feel and how much I felt the need to let it out. Dr. Leiva left it to me to decide what I wanted to talk about. I felt a little liberated every time after that. Only one problem was still absolutely unsolvable for me: my father. He started contacting me more often by phone or whatsapp. Most of the time he just wrote "Hello" and "How are you?"

I didn't respond to the attempts to make contact. But it upset me that he pretended nothing had happened. I couldn't deal with it and was angry every time he sent me another ridiculous message. I told Dr. Leiva about it and asked her how I should handle it. She said I should be honest with him and look for conversation. On the way home, I thought about it again. I decided to answer him even though I had a queasy feeling about it. But I knew I'd never feel free or would overcome the fear of confronting him with my past.

I wrote back in response to his succinct request that I was good. "And you?" I said.

He replied immediately that he was also well. That was it, and I got even angrier. A few days later he wrote another meaningless "Hello" and asked how I was. At the end, he wrote "I love you." I wish I'd jumped over the phone in rage and asked him if he even knew what love was. I pulled myself together and didn't answer him right away. I had to calm down first. I wrote him a few days later and reminded him of everything, from the moment he kidnapped me from the village and I believed that it was love and he was my savior. I remembered I'd had the last spark of confidence in him after the rapes by his stepson and how he had abused this trust. I told him that because of him I'd had trouble having a relationship because I've always been afraid of being lied to and abandoned. I told him I had become a control freak because of him and that I wanted to be perfect in everything I did. I looked in every person, who was close to me, after the lack of love for my father. And that I hurt others by scaring everyone with my kind. I told him I'd forgive him for anything, because my God did not allow me to continue living with this rage. I told him that I needed his love back then. I, finally, had the power to decide on my feelings. Only now did I know what I had accomplished in my life, despite the difficult times and experiences, I always stood up and kept fighting, because God didn't give up on me. And no matter what I did he always showed me the way back to life. He led my mistakes before my eyes. I told my father that he'd been one of those mistakes, because my hatred and anger for him made me sick.

He replied, "My mistake was not talking to you when you came to me."

I replied, "Pray to God that he will forgive you for your deeds. I am free and leave all things to God, who will do justice."

A little while later, my brother told me that my stepmother had died in an inexplicable way at my half-sister (her daughter). I didn't quite know how to feel in this situation. Though I've hated her all these years, I still felt a deep sense of sadness. I expressed my sincere condolences to the family and meant it. And so ended another chapter in my life. I forgive my father, and after 20 years of war and a thousand unanswered questions I was finally free. I've learned that everything in life has its reasons. I've found my peace in the voice that spoke within me. I got my peace and freedom, which I have never known before, and my insight into the meaning of life.

My psychiatrist, Dr. Leiva, was my guardian angel. She left the Wyss Clinic a short time later and opened her own practice. So I also changed the practice and kept her as my therapist up to the present. I've learned a lot about myself through Dr. Leiva's therapy. I now know that no therapy can help if you don't want it; you won't accept the help and you don't implement it in everyday life. Above all, you have to believe in yourself, otherwise you will be disappointed. I found for myself that therapists don't pain for me and cannot change my destiny. Dr. Leiva helped me find my way and helped me to relieve my pain, but not to make it go away.

No man and no antidepressants were able to do that. Only the inner will. It didn't help until I was ready to get on with my job and the problems of my past. That's what I was most afraid of, that's why I've always avoided it in my life. So I got to know myself step by step. I've learned to look after myself. I've learned to love myself before I expect someone else to. I won my self-confidence and now I know what I'm worth. I want to live my life the way I want it to, and make myself no longer dependent on other people. I am 100% entitled to my person and my life and my past.

I know today you can never give up no matter how futile the situation appears. You have to think about tomorrow and know that everyone has the same value in life. It's clear to me today that no one can handle everything alone. That's why you have to seek help and accept it. And you have to believe, especially in yourself. I first had to figure out who I was, what I wanted, where I was going to go and what I was in this world for. I got to know my family anew and also my fellow men. I learned that I could take a lot of people and things that I used to think I needed.

I realized that I am free from my anger, my fear, my despair and my constant feeling of powerlessness. I got rid of that today! I was able to free myself from the 20 years of war in my head by confronting myself with what was happening to me and at the same time triggered anger in me. The worst part for me was the thought of forgiving my father and his family for what they've done to me and my family. But I knew I'd never be set free with what scared me the most with the people who have inflicted the most suffering on me. That was the hardest step in this liberation for me, to forgive my father for something he didn't even feel sorry for. But I did it anyway. Not for him, but for me and my conscience, because I didn't want my life to be like this anymore, like before the accident. I am now liberated and know that in the end.

HERZ FÜR AUTOREN A HEART FOR AUTHORS À L'ÉCOUTE DES AUTEURS MIA ΚΑΡΔΙΑ ΓΙΑ ΣΥΓΓΡ
HJÄRTA FÖR FÖRFATTARE UN CORAZÓN POR LOS AUTORES YAZARLARIMIZA GÖNÜL VERELIM SZÍ
CUORE PER AUTORI ET HJERTE FOR FORFATTERE EEN HART VOOR SCHRIJVERS TEMOS OS AUTO
ZÖINKÉRT SERCE DLA AUTORÓW EIN HERZ FÜR AUTOREN A HEART FOR AUTHORS À L'ÉCOU'
AÇÃO ВСЕЙ ДУШОЙ К АВТОРАМ ETT HJÄRTA FÖR FÖRFATTARE À LA ESCUCHA DE LOS AUTOF
AUTEURS MIA ΚΑΡΔΙΑ ΓΙΑ ΣΥΓΓΡΑΦΕΙΣ UN CUORE PER AUTORI ET HJERTE FOR FORFATTERE EEN F
YAZARLARIMIZ G   Z   ZÖINKÉRT SERCE DLA AUTORÓW EIN HERZ FÜR
    SCHRIJ   S C   AÇÃO ВСЕЙ ДУШОЙ К АВТОРАМ ETT HJÄRTA FÖF

The author

Thulani Tomose was born in South Africa and grew up there until her mother brought her to Switzerland when she was 13 years old. Her life is marked by traumatic experiences and heavy strokes of fate. Abuse, violence, drugs, a serious car accident are all part of it. She trained as a hairdresser and nursing assistant and as a single parent takes care of her six-year-old son.

Her strengths include listening and great empathy. Writing was and is a way for her to process things. Now she presents her first publication with her autobiography. The aim of these is to motivate other people. I write openly and in detail about my story. In addition to writing, she enjoys exercise and fitness. She lives with her son in Bern.

The publisher

*He who stops
getting better
stops being good.*

This is the motto of novum publishing, and our focus
is on finding new manuscripts, publishing them and
offering long-term support to the authors.
Our publishing house was founded in 1997, and since
then it has become THE expert for new authors and
has won numerous awards.

**Our editorial team will peruse each manuscript
within a few weeks free of charge and without
obligation.**

You will find more information about
novum publishing and our books on the internet:

www.novumpublishing.com

www.ingramcontent.com/pod-product-compliance
Lightning Source LLC
Chambersburg PA
CBHW030515100426
42813CB00001B/52